Out of Albania

Out of Albania

From the Memoirs of Lawrence O. Abbott

"A True Account of a WWII Underground Rescue Mission"

Edited by Clint Abbott

Out of Albania, From the Memoirs of Lawrence Abbott

By Lawrence O. Abbott, Edited by Clint Abbott

First Edition 2010

Printed in the United States of America

Published by Lulu Press.

ISBN 978-0-557-30335-9 (hardcover)
ISBN 978-0-557-30329-8 (tradepaper)

Published in honor of a work my Father, Larry Abbott, began 65 years ago. Also to keep the memory of this special time in the hearts and minds of my family: my Wife, Michelle, my Mother, Verda Bushen Abbott, my Sisters and their husbands, Holly and Ray Bauer, Lori and Phil Long, all our children: Bethanie (husband Dean), Jeff, Nathan, Matt, Aaron, Jamie (wife Kelly), Amy, Caroline and grand-children: Christopher, Dana and Jaxon.

Contents

Preface

I am honored and excited to share one of the truly unique stories that had occurred during World WarII. I am honored because this is a true story in which my Father, Sergeant Lawrence O. Abbott played a role in. I am excited because this story was "lost" to our family for many years; it wasn't until recently that we discovered that my Father had written a book that was never published. This has been an exciting experience for me to be able to review his manuscript and make it available in a published format for others to enjoy.

What makes this story so unique is the presence of 13 nurses, as American military women were not supposed to be in combat or behind enemy lines. I also found it interesting that of the 30 Americans, the 13 nurses were all Lieutenants and the 13 enlisted men were all Sergeants with the exception of one who was a Corporal. During their 62 day walk, it is interesting to see how well they worked together. Though they were men, and they may have thought they should lead the group, the men showed respect for the nurses whom were leading.

In publishing this story I have relied upon the typed-written manuscript that was prepared by a local newspaper writer, Allen Field Smith (Mr. Smith typed as my Father shared the story with him verbally and through my Father's hand written account).

I also used Father's hand written notes as a cross reference and was able to locate the actual names of the Albanian Partisans who helped them along with the actual names of the towns or villages they visited (the typed-written manuscript was produced in 1945 and used fictitious names and places for security purposes). I have also relied upon conversations I have had with some of those who were in the 807th MAES, whom are still living including: Agnes Jensen Mangerich, Harold Hayes, Jim Cruise, Willis Shumway, and Elna Schwant Krumm (Willis and Elna have recently passed away). Agnes Jensen Mangerich also wrote a book on this account in 1999 entitled, "Albanian Escape." Her book provided valuable cross referencing.

The contrast between that book and my father's book is that, "Albanian Escape" was written from a nurses' perspective and highlights much of the nurses' experience; whereas, my father's book is written clearly from an enlisted man's perspective and captures events, conversations, and thoughts that are not necessarily found in "Albanian Escape." During their walk in Albania it wasn't uncommon, upon approaching a village, to have the women billeted in one place while the men were taken to another nearby village for their overnight lodging. The two works truly compliment each other.

I did enjoy the format of "Albanian Escape" and have used a similar format in this book, such as: the date/time stamping at each location where possible, the similar use of maps, and some of the same photographs.

I put the story forward as my Father wrote it, with minor editing and supplying the actual names and locations that were not available before. I am producing this work with the idea of honoring my Father in finishing something he started so many years ago and to honor those who served with him as well as their surviving families.

The passengers and crew of Aircraft 42-68809, Sixty-first TC SQ, 314th TC Gp, were as follows:

Flight Nurses of 807th Medical Air Evacuation Squadron

Name	Age	Hometown
2d Lt. Gertrude Dawson	29	Pittsburg, Pennsylvania
2d Lt. Ann Maness	32	Paris, Texas
2d Lt. Jean Rutkowski	26	Detroit, Michigan
2d Lt. Elna Schwant	25	Winner, South Dakota
2d Lt. Lois Watson	25	Oaklawn, Illinois
2d Lt. Lillian Tacina	23	Hamtramack, Michigan
2d Lt. Pauleen Kanable	26	Richland Center, Wisconsin
2d Lt. Helen Porter	30	Hanksville, Utah
2d Lt. Ann Markowitz	25	Chicago, Illinois
2d Lt. Wilma Lytle	31	Butler, Kentucky
2d Lt. Frances Nelson	25	Princeton, West Virginia
2d Lt. Ann Kopsco	25	Hammond, Louisianna
2d Lt. Agnes Jensen	29	Stanwood, Michigan

Medics of the 807th Air Evacuation Squadron

T/Sgt. Lawrence O. Abbott	Newaygo, Michigan
T/Sgt. John P. Wolf	Milwaukee, Wisconsin
T/Sgt. Charles J. Adams	Niles, Michigan
T/Sgt. Robert A. Cranson	Sandy Creek, New York
T/Sgt. Raymond E. Ebers	Steelville, Illinois
T/Sgt. Harold L. Hayes	Indianola, Iowa
T/Sgt. Robert E. Owen	Walden, New York
T/Sgt. Charles F. Zeiber	Reading, Pennsylvania
T/Sgt. Paul G. Allen	Greenville, Kentucky
T/Sgt. James P. Cruise	Brockton, Massachusetts
T/Sgt. William J. Eldridge	Eldridge, Kentucky
T/Sgt. Gordon M. MacKinnon	Los Angeles, California
Cpl. Hornsby (802d MAES)	Manchester, Kentucky

Flight Crew

Pilot: 1st Lt. Charles B. Thrasher	24	Dayton, Florida
Copilot: 2d Lt. James A. Baggs	28	Savannah, Georgia
Crew Chief: Sgt. Willis L. Shumway	23	Tempe, Arizona
Radio Operator: Sgt. Richard Lebo	24	Halifax, Pennsylvania

Introduction

    The country of Albania has a long history, much of which I will leave to the reader to research. Anges Jensen Mangerich, in her book, "Albanian Escape," does a very nice job at covering some of this history. Her book and this book will be excellent companions for those interested in the story of the 807th MAES stranded in Albania during World War II.

    I found the following information credible and a good introduction to the country of Albania:

Albania has had a wave of ethnicities populating and ruling its land for centuries. The longest reign was held by the Ottoman Empire (Turkey) which had at one time, spanned three continents with twenty-nine provinces, Albania being one of them. The Ottoman Empire's reign was just over 600 years, from 1299 a.d. to 1922 a.d. Albania pronounced its independence in 1912.

After a few years of political turmoil, Albania became more steady as a nation under the rule of King Zog. He was born Ahmet Muhtar Bey Zogolli; however, after serving as Prime Minister, and then President, he became the proclaimed King of Albania in 1928 and changed his last name from Zogolli to Zog.

For years, King Zog had been supported by the Italian government; however, with the rise of Hitler's Nazi party in Germany, along with their advancing conquests, Mussolini of Italy wanted a similar path for Italy. Mussolini led Italy to an invasion of Albania in 1939, overthrowing the government and sending King Zog into exile.

Mussolini, in October of 1940, used his Albanian base to launch an attack on Greece, which led to the defeat of the Italian forces and the Greek occupation of Southern Albania in what was seen by the Greeks as the liberation of Northern Epirus. While preparing for the Invasion of Russia, Hitler decided to attack Greece in December of 1940 to prevent a British attack on his southern flank. Albanian bunkers were built during the Hoxha regime to prevent possible external invasions.

During World War II, the Party of Labour was created on November 8, 1941. With the intention of organizing a partisan resistance, they called a general conference in Pezë on September 16, 1942 where the Albanian National Liberation Front was set up. The Front included nationalist groups, but it was dominated by communist partisans.

In December of 1942, more Albanian nationalist groups were organized under Visar Kola. Albanians fought against the Italians while, during Nazi German occupation, Balli Kombëtar allied himself with the Germans and clashed with Albanian communists, which continued their fight against Germans and Balli Kombëtar at the same time.

With the collapse of the Mussolini government in line with the Allied invasion of Italy, Germany occupied Albania in September of 1943, dropping paratroopers into Tirana before the Albanian guerrillas could take the capital. The German army soon drove the guerrillas into the hills and to the south. The Nazi German government subsequently announced it would recognize the independence of a neutral Albania and set about organizing a new government, police, and military. Many Balli Kombëtar units cooperated with the Germans against the communists, and several Balli Kombëtar leaders held positions in the German-sponsored regime ("Albania: History", Wikipedia).

Albania was considered an extremely poor, if not the poorest, country in Europe during the Second World War. It had very few roads with which to travel. Because the Germans had occupied this country and were performing road checks, most people resisting them traveled in the mountains and very rural villages.

Much of Albania's topography is rugged mountain terrain, from which come five major rivers that can prove to be at times, impassable. Very few homes had modern conveniences (electricity and running water), and food during the war time was scarce. For those coming from a modern country, circa World WarII, to find themselves in Albania would seem like traveling backwards in time.

My Father, Larry Abbott, was an X-ray technician at an Army Corps Field near Tacoma, Washington. Then he went to Medical Administrative Officer Candidate School (OCS) at either, Camp Barkley, Texas or Carlisle Barracks, Pennsylvania. After a few weeks into the OCS class, he decided that it wasn't what he expected, and he resigned. From there he was sent to Bowman Field in Louisville, Kentucky.

Larry Abbott ("Little Orville") was a Sergeant, T-3 Surgical Technician. He, along with Bob Owen, Harold Hayes, and John Wolf were assigned to be Flight leaders. These four would refer to each other as Bro. Owen, Bro. Hayes and Bro. Wolf. However, Bob Owen decided that Larry Abbott would not be Bro. Abbott, but would be called Little Orville. This was because my dad frequently looked at situations differently than most people did. Nothing wrong, but different. My dad was shorter than the other three, and his middle name was Orville. So he became Little Orville (This was shared with me by Harold Hayes in a letter he wrote me, October 20, 2000).

The 807th left Bowman Field to go overseas on August 10, 1943. On September 4, 1943, the ship landed in Bizert, Tunisia. They were in a bivouac area for about 6 days, and then the 807th moved to Fochville, which is a suburb of Tunis. Towards the end of the month they were told they would move to Catania, Sicily, where their headquarters would be located. They would begin to evacuate the sick and wounded as soon as they relocated. The 807th MAES moved to Catania, Sicily the first week of October.

1 – A Memorable Flight

November 6, 1943, Saturday

Cantania, Sicily

Benton was down for the Bari flight and I was posted for Algiers. I wanted to go to Bari to pay up a $25.00 loan I had from Captain Phil Voit since the day before our 807th air evacuation transport squadron had sailed from the states and Benton rather fancied a run to Algiers where he might get a chance to do some looking around. Usually in air evacuation you take the flight you draw, no matter where it's booked. In the few weeks we had been overseas, we had taken the flights as they came, all in the day's work, Algiers, Corsica, Sicily, Italy. But this time Benton and I swapped. I'd seen all I wanted of Algiers. Our orders were never so strict that we couldn't make a change of that kind. It was simply routine business between Benton and me. Benton got his look at Algiers. I damn near swapped my life.

We have no ships of our own. All our flying is by the troop carrier command. They flew everybody and everything, from brass hats to paratroopers, and from tank parts to a crate of eggs. On the morning of November 6, 1943, our Bari unit, along with a similar detachment assigned to Grottaglie, put out by jeep for the Catania airport in Sicily to catch our plane. Catania, the main Sicilian port across the channel from Italy, is on the south east slope of Mt. Etna, and was at this time, the point from which our unit operated. The air field had formerly been used by the Italians and Germans and had been put back into use by our engineers after invasion. The hangars had been completely destroyed and army construction crews along with civilian natives were at work there every day. Reaching the port on that November morning, we found it blanketed by fog and no ships moving.

November 7, 1943, Sunday 07:30 a.m.

Again on the morning of the seventh we were directed to a C53 transport that was on the strip. We settled ourselves in the row of bucket seats along each side of the box-car fuselage and fastened safety belts for the take-off. But soon a young lieutenant came out to the plane and told us that the flight had again been called off. We learned that zero ceilings were reported at Grottaglie and Bari. Back at quarters we took some ribbing from the outfit, but if the troop carrier wasn't flying, there was nothing we could do about it.

November 8, 1943, Monday 08:15 a.m.

The next day we went through exactly the same performance, but this time the field operations officer cleared us. At 8:15 our pilot, Lt. C.B. Thrasher, a Florida boy, gunned the C53's engines and we began to roll. As the big ship smoothed out in flight and the Catania harbor and coastline dropped swiftly away from us, we loosened our belts and leaned back against the walls of the cabin, where the steady drone of the C53's engines came in waves of vibrations across our shoulders. To Grottaglie, the little chalk and clay quarry city on the instep of the Italian boot, about ten miles northeast of Taranto, was a two-hour run, and to Bari, up on the Achilles tendon, was about thirty more minutes of flying.

We had a party of thirty aboard. Thirteen army nurses, thirteen enlisted men (all air corps medics), pilot, co-pilot, crew chief and radio man from troop carrier. Our gang, with one exception, was from the 807th and had been together since the outfit assembled and trained at Bowman field, Kentucky. We found out later that the air crew had never before flown together and the pilot had flown from this particular ship only once before. But there in the cabin that morning the feeling was quite as if we were a group of commuters making our daily trip to work on the 7:15. The nurses, in their weather-proof coats of light blue, were seated among the men, most of whom wore slate green field jackets and the peaked flight hats with the gold and blue piping of the air corps. Nobody talked much. Some of the girls began games of solitaire; others had paper-bound editions of novels and were soon absorbed in their stories. Sgt. William L. Shumway, from Arizona, our crew chief, wearing a summer flying suit and an open sheep lined flying jacket, moved about the plane, spending part of the time with Sgt. Richard L. Lebo of Harrisburg, Pennsylvania at the radio desk in the forward compartment or going on into the nose to be with pilots.

Half an hour out of Catania the C53 was bucking a strong head wind, and heavy fog had closed about us. Good transport weather that we were pretty much used to. These Douglas transports, in the opinion of most the flying men I know, are the safest planes in the war. The C53, and the C47 that has now superceded it to a large extent, can come in on one engine, can take the bumps and the weather, and absorb punishment of all kinds, but like all transport, they go unarmored and unarmed, depending on keeping out of sight and contact with enemy craft. We had one Thompson sub-machine gun and thirty rounds of ammunition aboard.

Shortly after nine o clock, we were forced into an electrical storm and could hear the gusts of rain against the propellers.

However, we soon passed through the storm area and were once more droning our way through the fog blanket, completely alone in the world, if one cares to think about it that way. None of us did. Three of the enlisted men, Sgt's. Paul Allen of Kentucky, Charles Adams, from our outfit, Pfc. Gilbert Hornsby, a Kentuckian from the 802nd squadron, who was making a change of station to rejoin his unit, and two of the nurses, began playing a game of rummy on the floor of the ship. The girls next to me, Lt. Gertrude Dawson from Pennsylvania and Lt. Pauline Kanable of Wisconsin, were deep in their books. Others, men and nurses alike, lulled by the beat of the engines, were dozing in their seats. This was the scene presented to Lt. Thrasher when he came back to tell us that there was no ceiling at Grottaglie and we were continuing to Bari. What he didn't tell us then was that the storm had damaged our compass and that lighting had drawn blue flame and a curl of smoke from the radio. Lebo, in his little cubby, was reading a well-thumbed detective story pulp, and we were flying blind and lost in deep fog at about 9,000 feet. Making a quiet check of emergency equipment, Shumway found we had seven parachutes, 23 Mae Wests and a couple of rubber life rafts.

But only the air crew knew the score then. We were just taking the ride. Our work began when we had patients on board. The troop carrier took us up, flew us, and brought us down. They'd done it too many times for us to worry about whether there was ceiling at Grottaglie or not. The rain hit us again, a drenching downpour that streamed the windows at our backs and whipped in a grey haze from the wings. The rummy game on the floor went on. Here and there a bit of conversation sprang up and then drifted off to silence. Suddenly, we roared out into an opening in the fog and below us, and quite near, we could see a strip of coast line with the sea tumbling into white foam as the waves broke among black rocks. Then, as we watched, a savage twister struck the beach, wrenching up a column of water and making it look like the plume of a large fountain. Thrasher swung the C53 away from the shore and the fog again engulfed us. One of the boys sighed, "Nope," he said to no one in particular, "that isn't Bari."

We sat there, listening to the sturdy, deep throated engines, at times loud and resonant as the ship swam through lighter belts of the mist and again dulled as we plunged into pea soup that almost blotted out our wing tips. We were long past the thirty minute run to Bari; long past our flying time from Catania for the whole trip. We were beginning to wonder where we were, and getting a mild jolt out of the thought that we hadn't the faintest idea about our location. But we did know that there was a radio beam out of Bari and that we should be on it or picking it up shortly. Thrasher put an end to that comforting thought when he appeared suddenly in the cabin doorway.

"We're going down when we come to an opening," he said calmly. "It may come quick. Everybody be ready for a forced landing."

For a moment he met the eyes of us all. Then he was gone, closing the door quietly. The rummy game broke up; those napping roused themselves. We all got busy, very busy, with our belts in a silence that made even our breathing seem audible. Yes, a C53 is as safe a ship as any that flies, but --- there it was. A C53 would hardly float long enough for us to get out if we came down over sea and a C53 was never built to sit down on a mountain at flying speed if land was somewhere down below us in the murk. Hornsby's voice broke the silence.

"Suffering cats," he drawled disgustedly, "they can't do this to me! Seven days now I had been trying to get out of Catania and back to my outfit. The field is closed, there is no ceiling on the other end, and I get ordered to my seat by everybody from generals down to a cook's second helper. And now this man comes and says he's going to set us down just any old place!"

So now we knew the score. I hoped I had as good a poker face as the rest. Sitting in one row and looking at people in another row, people you have even chances of dying with. Your insides tensing up minute by minute against the thought of the crunch and grinding roar as your blind ship crashes against a mountain side. This twisted Hornsby's thought into a prayer that he spoke aloud – "Lord, don't let this happen to me---us!" Striving for power to show you can take it --- as good as the next one.

Jim Cruise, a south Boston Irishman on his first flight in air evacuation and one of his first anywhere, squirmed around in his belt to peer out into the fog.

"How's he going to land---when---when he can't see?" His voice cracked a little as nerves closed his throat on the last words.

"Automatic pilot," said Sgt. Allen, drawing a laugh that came and died with the suddenness of a burst from a machine gun. The big Kentuckian pushed his hands down between his knees and rubbed the palms slowly back and forth. Adams shot him a look.

"Like that flight you made from Algiers, huh?" he said. Paul was 19 and had come in badly shaken from a flight on which a storm had nearly driven the plane he was riding into the sea.

"You aren't kidding me any," Allen answered. Then a grin touched his round, boyish face. He thrust an arm out level with his shoulder. "Ship was close as that to water," he declared. "I was dying every turn the props made. But I still think that damn Peterson did it on purpose. Sure never thought I'd see dry land again."

"You haven't," somebody cracked, "who's seen any DRY land?" The C53's engines drilled on through the mist, now loud, now dull, like the long-drawn, uneven snoring of some ancient giant. As long as we had that sound in our ears we were O.K. Some of the girls went back to their games of solitaire. Were they moving the cards with monotonous regularity, as if not seeing them? What of it? They knew the score. Sgt. Bill Eldridge, another Kentucky boy, from Eldridgeville, began to hum, "I'm Walking the Floor over You." Some of us joined in; while others pleaded that the ragged harmony was dried up. But that helped to ease us all, I think. It was 11:30 a.m. and we'd been in our seats for more than three hours.

The plane was on its way down before we realized the fog had opened. We pressed our faces to the windows, eager for the first glimpse of ground. The mist thinned out to long streamers and between them we could see stretches of greenish brown land. Thrasher took us down to about two thousand feet and there, below us, was an airport.

We could count ten planes on the field, but the sight of them didn't cheer us much. Everybody started guessing. Some said Italian, others German. Shumway, the Crew Chief, peering from a window far back in the plane, spoke with some authority.

"Not Jerry," he said. "And not ours," added Allen, gloomily.

That made them Italian. But who cared? We were out of the clutches of the fog. We had a landing spot made to order. We hadn't hit the mountains. We were coming down alive. The rest didn't seem to matter a lot. Allen was muttering to himself, "What are we waiting for? Go on in! Make up your mind, fella!"

Thrasher had been cruising the C53 around the field in lowering circles. He made three trips and then, on the fourth, he straightened her out and started her in. I could see the field. And then, out of the corner of my eye I saw what looked like sparks shooting out of the tail of our plane. Things happened so fast then that no one had time to think. Those sparks were tracer bullets, pouring up at us from the ground. We heard several bursts of heavier stuff. Up in the pilot's cabin, Thrasher jammed his throttles far into the red sector of the dial. The C53's engines screamed wide open as we clawed our way up and out of there a lot faster than any C53 was built to climb. Below, on the field, several fighter planes darted along the strip into the air. The fog closed again around us and we welcomed it now, as the arms of a friend. Up and up we went until Thrasher was satisfied had had gained a safe altitude. We saw nothing of the fighters. The excitement loosened our tongues.

"So now we get shot at," announced Hornsby. "Where are we?" asked Lt. Ann Markowitz, a Chicago girl and a member of our 807th since the Bowman field days.

"The sixty-four-dollar question," declared New Yorker Bob Owen. "All we know is that those boys back there were hostile. And I mean --- ."

"We must be up around Rome somewhere," interrupted J. P. Wolf from Glidden, Wis., "anyhow back of the German lines."

"Bet a fin we ain't within a hundred miles of Rome," said Adams. "Italian planes and Italian gunners, but ---."

"Yeah, chimed in Allen, "and they don't shoot for our sour apples. Here we come, slow and big as a house---boy! If they'd been Yanks, we'd be on the ground right now---in pieces."

"Noon-hour," said Ebers, who liked to talk about his home in Illinois, "everybody out to lunch. That sure saved our bacon."

"So what?" asked Zieber, the boy from Reading, Pa., who never believed his luck would hold. It brought us to a sudden silence in which the fog was no longer friendly and the drone of the C53's engines became a haunting wail.

2 - Landing On Our Nose

November 8, 1943 – Monday 1:00 p.m.

Welcome to Albania

Owen was fretting about his German Mauser pistol. He'd left the gun with our supply sergeant and there seemed to have been an understanding between them that it was to be the property of the HQ man until Bob returned to claim it.

"He'll sell it, he'll lose it in a crap game, he'll get it stole off him, he'll trade it or hock it, maybe he'll send it home. Dumbest thing I ever done! Should've stuck it right in my musette. That's the one thing I sure want to ------."

"Fog's thinning out," somebody broke in.

We were in another hole of comparatively clear air and starting down. But we hadn't gone far before Thrasher nosed up and took us back into the murk. Shumway came back from up front where he had been spending a few minutes with the pilots.

"What's the matter now?" asked Hornsby, peevishly. "Doesn't this guy ever get tired of playing peek-a-boo?" Shumway gave him a look. "Just a flight of four Messerschmitts out looking for trouble," he said. Hornsby grunted. "Well," he countered, "I guess WE would not have given them any trouble."

"That's right," said Shumway. I almost asked him how the gas stood, but bit my mouth shut just in time. That was the question that was looming in everyone's mind now. The old C53 had been pushed around a lot on this trip; headwinds, storm, a lot of climbing, rain, and fog. When those engines began to cough and spit, we could count the minutes we had to live on the fingers of our hands. But they kept going strong as the slow minutes ticked away. We sat and waited in dogged silence, trying to hang onto our nerves as the tension mounted. You get so you can't just sit there staring at the person opposite you and have him staring back. I twisted around to look out the window, fixing my eyes on the broad, brown spread of the C53's wing. Pretty soon I was sure I could see ice beginning to form out there. If I was right, our number was up. In the fog we were as good as dead; all thirty of us. I'd heard stories about how fast ice could build up and how quick it can take a ship down. This didn't seem to be coming on very fast, and even as I watched, the mist turned to streamers again and we hit our third opening.

Thrasher put the big ship into a power dive. First time down that way for me, and I'm perfectly satisfied to have it the last. I thought that express elevator feeling was going to black me out, and could feel the muscles of my face drawing into taut, hard lines. But at last we leveled out and there below us was an open field, flanked by brush covered hills. At one end of the field, there was a small lake, bordered by what appeared to be mud flats.

Settling into the valley, our C53 cruised over a tight circle while Thrasher studies his landing. Shumway moved aft from the pilot's compartment, cautioning us to check our belts. He then took his station just ahead of the baggage section in the tail of the ship, getting a grip on the wall of the tiny lavatory room and the fuselage, bracing himself as best he could for the shock of landing.

We felt the ship dip as Thrasher started her in and I took a glance out the window. The ground was close, sickeningly close and streaming under us a terrific speed. The C53 lands normally at about 95 miles an hour. This was bringing in a flying box car and setting on ground you had never touched before close to a hundred! Suddenly, somehow, we got a God-sent stall that clipped perhaps thirty miles from our speed. Then we hit. It was as pretty a three-pointer as I've ever been in. The tired old C53 lurched and waddled along over the rough ground, dipping her wings, creaking in all her joints from the furrowed stubble of the field. Then we experienced a terrific jolt forward and the tail swung up. I don't know what happened to the rest, but I died right there. Only instead of going on over, the tail flopped back down again and almost instantly we came to a stop with a suddenness that threw us against our belts.

At that moment we caught a flash of Shumway sailing through the air in the position of a broad jumper at the peak of his leap, knees bent, hands thrust forward. Streaming behind him our musette bags, a metal tool box and other sundry equipment were flung into the air. The crew chief sprawled onto the floor, pelted by almost everything that was loose in the baggage space. He scrambled to his feet, staggered over to the door, opened it and fell out onto the ground. We tore our belts loose and followed him as fast as we could make it, on the rule of clearing ship as quickly as possible after a forced landing because of the danger of fire.

For a few moments we all huddled around the plane, finding out that we could draw our breath and that our hearts had not stopped permanently. Nobody paid attention to what was said or done. We were too glad to be alive. We didn't even notice the rain that was pouring on us. But somebody did notice Shumway, lying in the mud, too groggy to get up. We picked up the injured crew chief and laid him on a tail surface of the plane. The nurses got busy then. He had small cuts on his face and neck, but the worst spot was in his left knee, a deep, round hole, looking like a nail had been driven into it. Two of the girls also needed patching for cuts on their faces.

While the gauze and tape were being applied from first aid kits, Lt. Thrasher and Second Lieutenant J.A. Baggs, our co-pilot from Georgia, moved to the front of the plane where they fished cigarettes from their flying jackets and began to take stock of our situation. Those of us who were not busy with our three casualties gradually joined the pilots. Baggs seemed hard hit by the loss of the plane. Again and again he moved about to touch some part of it, talking to the ship as if it had been something alive, and there were tears in his eyes as he spoke. He showed us the places where the bullets from the enemy field had ripped through the wings. It had been that close, but the C53 had brought us through. Back along our tracks in the sloppy surface of the field we could see a low stump, accounting for the jolt that had flipped the transport up onto its nose. The landing gear was now bedded into the soft mud at the edge of the flats bordering the lake. It was plain that the stump had broken Shumway's grip and we'd hit the mud before he had a chance to recover.

The rain drummed loud on the big quiet plane and we stood ankle deep in the ooze as we looked about the valley. As far as we could see there was not a house, not a creature moved; the land lay silent and brooding in every direction, only the ploughed stubble under foot giving evidence of habitation.

"O.K.," Thrasher said, flipping away his soggy cigarette, "let's get going. There's a shack up there on the hill a way. I don't think there's anybody in it, but we might as well start getting the bad news."

We carried Shumway back into the plane and the nurses and all but four of the enlisted men moved back into the ship to get out of the wet. Then our little party of six, the two pilots, Allen, Adams, Harold Hayes from Indianola, Iowa, and I, started trudging through the rain for the hillside. At the edge of the field we came to a curious fence built of brush, crossed it, and were working our way up the rough, wooded slope when we heard shouting behind us. Part of the group back at the plane was out, waving their arms and yelling for us to come back. Then on the opposite hill we saw a number of roughly clad men moving down towards the ship. We double-timed back, picked up several more of the boys as we passed the C53 and went on to meet friend or foe. Within a short distance Thrasher ordered Eldridge to go back and bring our Thompson gun and ammunition. Then, quickly realizing that we couldn't put up any sort of fight and that shooting would simply endanger the lives of us all, he countermanded the order and told Bill to have them break out some white as a sign of surrender.

In the fog and rain, we couldn't make much of the men on the hillside until we came closer to them. By this time the party at the C53 was out, the girls waving white handkerchiefs and the men spare undershirts taken from their musettes. The men on the hill converged on us and as we met we saw they were natives of some sort, clothed in threadbare cloaks and baggy trousers and armed only with mattocks, short axes, and big knives. One, a blond-bearded chap of about twenty five, appeared to be the leader. We tried him in the few phrases of French and Italian we knew, but made no headway beyond a general shaking of their heads. Thrasher then asked them if they were German and made the sign of the swastika for them. This they seemed to understand and heads were nodded vigorously. Baggs shrugged his shoulders. Then he set his rain-soaked garrison cap more firmly on his head.

"Well sir," he remarked, "seems like this man's war is plumb over for we-all."

3 – Americans Meet Albanian Partisans
November 8, Monday – 1:30 p.m.
807th Aided By Albanian Patriots

Even as the co-pilot spoke, more shouting broke out, this time from the direction of the lake, and we could see a half-dozen or more men running around the shore and heading for the plane. So we plowed our way back through the mud to meet them. As they drew nearer we could see that they carried rifles and were in uniform of some sort. Long before they reached us we understood the word they were shouting "Americano, Americano!" We managed to intercept them before they reached the plane. They came up with broad smiles on their bearded faces, greeting us with hugs and hearty hand-shakes, some of them even trying to kiss us. We gave them some of our cigarettes on which they puffed with appreciation that amounted almost to reverence, drawing the smoke deep into their lungs and pulling on the butt until it burned their fingers. Over and over they repeated the word, "Americano!" We called them "kammerad", which seemed to please them immensely. Men were pouring out of the hills on the both sides now and there was quite a crowd around the plane. Some were in uniform and had rifles, as those that had some along the lake; while others were in peasant garb as those we had first met.

"Those uniforms are Italian or I'm crazy," someone said, voicing the thought uppermost in our minds. Who were these people? Where had we landed? We seemed to be among friends, but what was to happen to us was not yet clear.

"Some of these boys got German coats on," Owen declared. "And look at those guns. There's hardly two alike in the lot."

It was beyond us. But, when we tried to press them with questions, framed as best we could in sign language, all we got was the word "commandant." Then they'd point in the direction we had taken on first leaving the plane. We had to be satisfied with that. The commander of the group, whoever they were, was evidently coming to meet us.

"Well," said Thrasher, "here's hoping the guys speaks some kind of talk we can go along with."

Soon a man riding a small white horse with brown markings appeared in the brush on the hillside, rode down to the fence where he dismounted and then came across the field toward us. This was the "commandant." Baggs walked out alone to meet him. As they came close the man halted, brought his closed fist to his eyebrow and said something. Baggs responded with a snappy American salute. They shook hands and together, came walking back to the plane.

Under the wing of the big transport, while we all clustered around, the leaders held a conference. The man could speak English. In response to our eager questions he laughed and told us we were in Albania. He introduced himself as Hassan Jina. He was the leader of the band of patriot guerillas now grouped around us.

We judged that Hassan was young, most likely in his early twenties. He had dark hair and eyes, a black handle bar mustache, and was wearing the uniform of an Italian solider. He had on a grey-blue uniform coat of some kind, which was open, and on his feet were a pair of heavy rubber boots. His voice was low-pitched and, speaking English, the words came slowly, sometimes halting altogether while he groped for a way to express his meaning. His favorite phrase, and one he seldom inserted at the right point, was "Never mind."

Hassan told us that he had recognized the plane as American by the huge white star pained on the fuselage. Riding his white horse out on the hill where his followers could see him, he said, was the signal for them not to shoot at the plane. He could not get over his assumption that we were paratroopers, spearheads of a big invasion force the Allies were to put into Albania. His eyes kept roving the plane, evidently searching for armament of some kind, and he kept asking us about our guns. While we talked, the patriot soldiers and peasants stood in a silent ring about the ship, staring stolidly at the little group under the wing, or following with their eyes the nurses as the girls moved back and forth between the parley, in which they were intently interested, and the shelter of the cabin. Hassan addressed himself mostly to Baggs, apparently taking the co-pilot's garrison cap as the badge of command. Baggs and Thrasher, between them, finally made it clear that while we were a part of the American army, we were, as far as we knew, the only part of it now in Albania. Then they asked him where the Germans were. Hassan nodded his head slowly and tweaked his long mustache as he pondered his reply.

"The Germans," he began slowly, "are all around." A wide sweep of his arm accompanied the words, and a chill of silence settled over us as we waited for him to go on. "The Germans," he repeated, "go to this place, and then they go to another place. They take all the food, the corn, the goats; they burn one, two, three, sixes houses. They stay one day, two days, never mind, but five days, and then they go back. But we kill some."

Hassan looked down at his boots. Then he laughed. "Po, po, po, yes, yes," he said, in his deep voice, "We kill some."

We looked at Hassan. Then our eyes went out to his silent men in their mixed uniforms, who stared back at us through the rain. So that was it. These were the hardy fighters of Albania we'd read and heard about. They didn't draw their stuff from QM. When they wanted a coat or a pair of boots or a gun, they went out and killed a Jerry or two who had what they wanted.

"Roger," Thrasher nodded. He fumbled for a cigarette and shoved the pack at Hassan. "Well," he continued, "we're your babies. We don't want the Germans to get us. You've got to help us. We want to get back to Italy, see?"

Hassan blew a long streamer of smoke. "You are Americano," he replied slowly, "good for us. We like Americano. Never mind. The Germans do not take you from us. We help you. But Italy ---- that is many days. We go first to our city ---- Berat."

Going to a place we'd never heard of, guided by men we'd never seen. But Thrasher had no choice. "All right," he agreed, "let's go. How far is it?"

Hassan nodded. "For us," he said, "two days, but for you I think four."

"Kick me, Orville," said Adams, who was standing next to me, "I must be dreaming. This Albania isn't even a good sized postage stamp on an ordinary map and this guy says it'll take us four days to get to a town. Why in four days a guy can around the world!"

But we were no longer in air transport. Everything seemed to be settled but it still took a lot of talking and planning. The rain still pelted the wing above us and the wet had long since soaked through our shoes as we stood there listening to the conference. The ring of people around the ship broke up as some of the soldiers moved in for a closer examination, stopping now and then to peer through the windows into the dusk of the cabin where Shumway, stretched out on the floor, had been made as comfortable as possible. The rest of our group was ranged around the plane in the bucket seats, a few constantly coming and going to keep the less restless ones on the inside informed on what was taking place.

3:30 p.m. – A Shack on the Hillside

At last the plans were made and we were ready to move. Hassan was taking us to a house about a two hour walk, back in the hills where we could spend the night. Shumway was to be taken to a stable and servants quarters, only a short distance away, and then be brought on by ox cart. We were all told to gather up equipment from the plane, taking as much of the necessary and useful stuff as we could manage. Hassan's soldiers carried some of the things for us, and we got almost everything that was loose, including parachutes, Mae Wests, and the two deflated life rafts. We tore out a section of bucket seats to make a litter for Shumway, using the two blankets we had for padding and covering for the crew chief. Hassan brought in his horse and insisted that Baggs get into the big, uncomfortable looking wooden saddle and ride the animal at the head of the section setting out directly for the house. Hassan himself was going with us. The commandant's horse with one party and the commandant with the other placed the official stamp of approval on both groups.

It was after three o'clock and there was no let up in the rain as the first section set off, slogging away through the mud, Baggs brown leather flying jacket bobbling with the motion of the horse at the head of the file and the nurses, in their blue-green field coats with the parkas drawn up over their heads, following after. A detail of Hassan's men brought up the rear. They moved on past a big tree, over the hill trail we had planned to take to find the shack Thrasher had spotted from the plane before landing. We turned back to our job.

Shumway kicked about being carried and swore he could walk with his arms on the shoulders of a couple of men, but those of us who had seen the hole in his knee knew different and besides we had orders to carry.

"Shut up and get on this thing," somebody told him, "we want to haul tail out of here."

Shumway permitted himself to be placed on the litter.

"You guys are lucky," he declared. "I only weigh 177 now. Before the army took me I was 235."

We pushed off with our loads. Hornsby, making a change of station, had a barracks bag full of stuff, but the rest of us only our musettes. Behind us, people swarmed over and around the C53. Thrasher, knowing it would never take the air again, had given permission for them to dismantle it, and they lost no time going to work. I was glad that Baggs was not there to see it, and I think we all felt a twinge of regret, hearing the thump of axes and the sharp clink of metal on metal behind us. We were really on foot now. The patriots had promised to camouflage what was left of the plane. We were all heavily hung with equipment we hoped to salvage. Lebo had the ships compass, and, with others relieving him from time to time, was also toting the dead radio set.

After about half an hour we came to a low stone building that appeared to be very old. We carried Shumway through the doorway into a darkened room in which the stench of cattle mingled with smoke from a small fire that stung our eyes. As soon as possible we went outside again where we found Hassan and several peasants yoking a pair of oxen into an ancient looking cart with two massive wooden wheels. We loaded Shumway on his litter, into the cart, hung our bags and as much other equipment as we could over the stakes sticking up form the sides, and moved off again through the rain.

"Air evacuation by ox cart," scoffed Sgt. Gordon MacKinnon, a former forest ranger. "I bet Bowman field will blow up a storm if they ever get word of this."

Mac stopped to light a cigarette in the soggy, chill wind that was beginning to cut through our drenched flight jackets and make us miserable with cold.

"And I'll bet there'll be high mass for us tonight," Owen commented.

At times we seemed to be following a faint cart track, and again it was definitely just plain brush country. We were working our way along the side of the mountain, sometimes climbing for a short distance and then dropping down grade again. The oxen swayed slowly along at their tireless pace, now and then tossing their heads and blowing their breath in a cloud of soft steam into the cold air. We trudged along in the mud behind them. The driver and Hassan walked beside the beasts, perfectly at ease, never hesitating about the way, and we gave them blind confidence.

Dusk was deepening as we came out of the woods and into an opening where a rambling sort of house stood. We moved past a large tree that stood out by itself in the clearing and then came to a halt at the foot of a flight of stairs leading up to the second story of the house. Above, on the landing and along the narrow porch on that side of the house, several of the nurses stood, watching us. We carried Shumway up those stairs and at the top the girls told us we were supposed to take off our shoes before we went into the room assigned to us. We didn't know what to make of it. They knew the score too well to be putting up a rib on us.

"Says which?" somebody piped.

"You have to take off your shoes before you go in," one of the nurses repeated, "It's an old Albanian custom."

"What, they have gold carpets?"

"You'll see," was the cryptic answer, "but haul out of your shoes."

So we took off our rain soaked, mud daubed brogans and marched in.

"And I'm going in with my boots on," Shumway pointed out.

The room was small and filled with smoke from a fire burning on a little rectangular hearth of stone raised about three inches off the floor. It was flanked by two narrow, tightly shuttered window openings and between these a dip in the wall, blackened with soot, led up to the ceiling. There was no chimney outlet of any kind. By the time we were all inside there was hardly more than standing room. We took turns getting in front of the fire to get warm and make a start at drying our clothes, but the smoke was almost more than we could bear, although we kept the door part way open.

The room became more crowded as the boys who had been stowing the rest of our baggage came in. There was no furniture of any kind. On the floor were a few strips of old carpet which did little to keep the cold and damp from coming up into our feet. Darkness closed in and the feeble light of the fire set dim shadows flickering along the walls. We draped ourselves about the place as best we could, a pretty quiet company. There wasn't much to say and there was a lot to think about. In one part of the room Baggs and Hassan were carrying on a conversation about the final disposition of the plane. Hassan wanted the ship burned and, of course Baggs was against it. The talk went on and on, the Albanian's low voice and slow sentences mingling with the rapid flow of the co-pilot's Georgia accent. Some of it was probably funny, but nobody did any laughing. Our minds were primarily occupied with taking stock of our surroundings and casting ahead as to what the outcome might be for us. It wasn't a pretty picture from where we sat just then. Baggs at last raised his voice in an appeal to Thrasher.

"Are we going to let them burn our ship?" he asked a note of pleading in his voice. Thrasher, hugging his shins as he sat on the floor in front of the fire, hardly turned his head as he answered.

"She's no good to us, Jim. She'll never fly again. Don't you get it? If the Jerries find it they'll kill some of these people to make them give information about us. If it's nothing but a charred heap, why we crashed and burned and that's all they know. We ought to burn it tonight."

Baggs drew a deep breath.

"O.K." he said. Then his voice rose, "But I'm the man that does it!" He still seemed to be thinking of the C53 as he would a favorite horse when he added, "I'll put her out of the way."

They rounded up a few flashlights. Baggs stuffed flare gun cartridges into his pockets. Then, with the mixed group of our fellows and patriots, he set off down the mountain. They made much better time than we did, but it seemed hours before they got back. They'd soaked the ship with gasoline from the tanks and then Baggs, standing back, had fired five flares into it, only to have them sputter and go out in the rain. Each of the enlisted men had tried a shot. Not one had caught. The C53 refused to burn. One of the boys said that Jim Baggs had been crying as he got the flares off. "And I was feeling pretty damn low myself," he admitted.

Allen, who had been with the party, pushed his way in close to the fire, spreading his arms wide as if to draw the heat into his big body.

"Boy!" he said his voice loud in the stuffy little room, "when do we eat?"

"Shut up," somebody said, "what's that going on outside?"

A low rumble, not thunder, could be heard and a bunch of us got up and went out. On the horizon we could see a maze of tracer bullets and flashes of flack in the night sky. Then there were lower bursts of flame. Hassan had followed us out.

"The English," he said quietly from the darkness, "are paying the Germans a little call with bombs. The Germans do not never mind like it."

He laughed softly.

"Now," he said, "we get you something to eat."

Hassan made good. Within a few minutes a peasant woman entered the room bringing us our introduction to Albanian corn bread, crusty flat cakes, tasting slightly sour. How we learned to hate that corn bread! But tonight we were hungry. Johnny Wolf, sitting next to me sank his teeth into one of the cakes, breaking off a big bite which he chomped with gusto.

"Not food for a king, son," he observed, "but right now I could eat a muskrat with the hair on!"

I expect a couple of the nurses choked on that one, but they were hungry too and kept right on with our late supper. Pretty soon the woman came back with what we took to be some boiled chicken. The few bites I had tasted all right and helped the meal along a lot. It must have been quite a delicacy, brought on as a special honor for us. Hassan came to tell us that his men were on guard for the night. Then we were left, all thirty of us, to settle down as best we could.

Probably we all slept some. We were plenty tired. But there was never a time, I'm sure, when more than half of us were asleep, so it amounted to sleeping in shifts. I found a place near the door. It was cold there, but the smoke was not so bad. Sitting with my back to the wall, legs stretched out in front of me, I could see the silhouettes of some of the nurses, seated before the fire, cradling in their laps the heads of the girls who were lying on the floor. Now and then one of the nurses would get up and go over to see how Shumway was making it. All around the shadowy room men were stretched out, everybody too tired to do any more talking. Those of us who happened to be awake, were busy with our thoughts.

I was thinking of how swift and complete had been the change that had come to us in the last few hours. Only this morning we'd had breakfast, a good American army breakfast, at our own quarters in Sicily. All this couldn't be real. This couldn't be happening to a kid from Newaygo, Michigan. Home was at least six thousand miles away, maybe more than that. It was too far for me to ever get back. Tired, so wet --- so cold ---

"You awake, Orville?" said a voice in the darkness near me. It was Wolf, speaking hardly above a whisper.

"Hell, yes," I grunted.

"I've been thinking'," He said, hunching himself closer, "this ought to be good rabbit country. Why not? Judas! If we could just kick out a few rabbits, huh? Boy, would they go good!"

"Nuts," I growled, "there isn't anything in this lousy country."

"Let's sneak out as soon as it's light and take a look," Wolf urged.

"O.K." I didn't want to talk about it. It must have been ten minutes later I heard John mutter "rabbits." Then he stirred a little and sighed in his sleep. I caught several naps through what seemed to be an endless night, then Wolf was shaking my arm gently and, opening my eyes, I saw the partly open door outlined in gray. We went outside quietly, and found Allen and Owen already out.

"Hey," Paul said in greeting, "you birds got any cigarettes?"

My hand moved towards my pocket. Then I stopped. A queer feeling, this thought that I was carrying what was apt to be my last pack of American cigarettes in a long time.

"The same to you and many of them," I said, getting very tough. But I couldn't go through, standing there blowing smoke at them. I pulled out the pack and doled one cigarette to each man. "Don't forget, I'll sure put the mooch on you," I warned.

"Hornsby's got a couple cartons in his barracks bag," Allen assured me, as he lighted up. "Say," he went on, "do you know we're prisoners? You've got to get permission from these guys to go find yourself a spot in the bushes. There isn't but the one can in the whole place, up there on the side porch and I suppose we ought to leave that to the women. It isn't anything but a slot in the floor anyhow. Now right up there, gentlemen, is the family wash room. Soap and towels is extra and there isn't any."

Paul pointed to the roofed over porch between the two wings of the house, reached by a flight of steps that landed not far from where we stood. The porch was supported on stout, rough hewn posts, and beneath was an open space where stock could be tied, the ground being heavily littered with straw. Wolf and I went up the steps and found the wooden kegs of water with a couple of copper pitchers and some copper basins beside them on the floor. J.P. picked up one of the basins and was about to fill it at one of the kegs when Hassan spoke from behind us.

"No, no, no, not like that. I show you."

Hassan was in the doorway of the wing opposite to the one in which we had spent the night, a room that was used as a kitchen. Stepping across the porch to us, he picked up a pitcher and filled it from a keg. Then he placed a basin on the floor and motioned me to him. He began pouring the water in a thin, long stream into the basin.

"Now," he said, "never mind, wash, make fast, wash, wash, while I am pouring for you."

I rubbed my hands under the trickle of icy water, cupped them and tossed water over my face and around my neck. It felt good, scattering that sleep-doped feeling. I finished up army-style by running my dripping hands through my hair. Then I remembered Paul had said there were no towels. Hassan set the pitcher down and beamed while I stood there with the cold drops running down my neck.

"That is how," he said. Wolf eyed the process with disapproval.

"Hell," was his only comment. He grabbed a pitcher, filled it, poured himself a basin of water and then proceeded to wash like a threshing hand. Hassan only shrugged and went down the steps. The point was that the water in the kegs was used for both washing and drinking. That was why you always dipped with the pitchers. We went back down the stairs, drying ourselves as best we could.

More rain had fallen during the night and the ground under foot was mushy. The air seemed to drip with moisture, the sky was hung with low, heavy clouds and there seemed little prospect of it clearing. A few chickens and several turkeys were scratching about in the straw under the porch. Over all was the brooding silence of the land, the quiet we had noticed when our plan had come to rest in the little valley. Off about fifty yards in front of the house was a small lake, its brush-lines shore vague in the dawn mist.

November 9, 1943, Tuesday - Early Morning

As day came on, members of our party began to come out on the porch. The girls gathered around the kegs, carrying on their washing Albanian style, as if they had been used to it all their lives. They talked among themselves, occasionally sending a burst of hearty American laughter out on the quiet morning air. Lt. Jean Rutkowski, from Detroit, had a small overnight case with a mirror fitted into the top of it. They propped the case up on the edge of one of the kegs and went right ahead with powder and make-up just as though they were in the ladies room at the Ritz. They took that Albanian dawn like the real sports they proved to be all along the way.

There was nothing for us to do except to stand around and see what was going to happen next. Word of our arrival had evidently spread through the hills by the grapevine and people began coming in to see us. After a while we had some breakfast. More corn bread, made into a somewhat sour sort of mush with what somebody said was goat's milk. Then there was a little cheese, a stringy sort of stuff that all but gagged us. We gave it a hearty GI gripe.

"One more meal like this," somebody said, "and we better send for the Jerries to come and get us."

"Don't let Hassan hear that kind of talk," Thrasher said sharply. "And let's try to remember that these people are doing the best they can for us."

He was right, of course, but just then we were in no mood to agree with him.

Hassan told us that a "big man" was coming to see us and make plans for our escape from Albania. Meanwhile, as the morning passed, more people, soldiers and peasants, drifted in. Among them were some Albanian women soldiers. They had uniform coats that we judged were Italian, knee-length skirts of rough, wooly cloth, wrap leggings, and the heavy, felt, slipper-like shoes such as were worn by most of the natives. Only one of the women wore uniform britches. She was the one who sang "Tonight We Love" in English, for our nurses. They seemed never to get enough of staring at the American girls in their belted field coats and parkas. Those coats were the ones the girls had kicked to high heaven about wearing, but for which we all returned thanks before our first week in Albania was over. They had detachable linings which the nurses often took out and loaned to us when the wind cut through our field jackets. They did shed rain and keep the girls fairly dry.

At eleven o'clock word came that the patriot leader, (Hassan's superior), was approaching. Soon he came in sight along the way we had traveled the night before. He rode proudly up to the house between the two respectfully silent files of his people and dismounted from his bay horse with a flourish that was comical. Then he marched up to Trasher and Baggs, who were standing in the stable space under the porch with Hassan. Again we saw that strange salute, and this time we heard the words.

"Vedekee Faschishme!" was what it sounded like, and we later learned it mean "death to Fascism!"

Hassan's closed fist touched his eyebrow. "Liri Populi!" ---- "Live the people!" said he. All over Albania that is the greeting. They don't say hello, or good morning, or how are you, good-bye or good night. They say "Death to Fascism!" men, women, and children, alike, and they really mean it.

The new leader made a short speech to our officers. Hassan translated it. We were welcomed to Albania and assured that we would be safe among the patriots. Then, with Hassan's help, a conference began. The Germans, we learned, kept pretty much to the valleys where they had air fields and had garrisoned a number of larger towns. In the hills and mountains the patriots were in control, except for occasional forays such as Hassan had mentioned the previous evening. There was a British agent somewhere in our vicinity, but his exact whereabouts at this time was not known. Word of us would be sent to him immediately and he would be asked to help. Yes, his Albanians could furnish us with some mules to transport our injured one, and some who perhaps needed to ride (a glace toward nurses, who were interested listeners) and to carry our baggage. No, we didn't have mules for everybody; but we did have some mules, poh, poh, poh, yes.

At this point Lt. Jean Rutkowski took off an extra GI wrist watch she had and handed it to Thrasher to give to the leader. C.B. made the presentation through Hassan.

"Why don't you put it on for him; show him how it goes," the pilot suggested. Rutkowski walked forward, her hand out, palm up;

and gave the "big man" a bright smile. But the Albanian didn't understand. She had to take the watch from him and then show that she wanted him to hold out his arm while she strapped it to his wrist. With the watch in place, she cupped her hands over the dial, showing him it was luminous. The patriot's ruddy face lighted with amazement and pleasure. The Detroit girl patted the watch, gave him a smile and nod, and then stepped back to her place among the nurses. Immediately, the Albanian cupped his hand over the watch, stared at it a moment, and then, looking up, began to shout. He ran to a dark corner under the porch and his people followed him like an excited mob. It broke up the parley for fifteen minutes. While his followers pressed closely about him, the leader proudly displayed the luminous dial of the watch. To them it was magic.

Out in the yard some of us gathered around the leader's horse, looking with almost as much amazement at the Albanian saddle. It was made entirely of wood with no adding of any kind. Two saplings, hewn or whittled flat had been bent into bow shaped pieces fitting down over the animals' back, and between them ran a number of horizontal slats. That's all there was to it, except for wooden pegs on which to hang things. To us it was the craziest, most clumsy looking excuse for a saddle any of us had ever seen.

"I still just don't believe it," was the verdict given by Jim Baggs, after a thorough inspection. The stirrups were simply loops of rope. There was no saddle blanket and the horse was evidently controlled only by a halter rope. We later learned that the Albanians almost never use bitted bridles, guiding their steeds by flicking a little switch along the side of the head opposite to the way they wish to turn.

When the leader got through showing off his watch, Hassan made us a speech, responding to the gift.

"He says because we love the Americans and are glad they have come to Albania never mind," he declared with solemn dignity, "we now kill cattle and have a feast."

"Yippee!" yelled Johnny Wolf, flourishing a fat bladed hunting knife he'd bought the other day before we sailed from the States. "I'm the butcher boy from Butcherville! Just lead me to that critter!"

Somebody said it was a water buffalo they brought out to slaughter. The beast was led to the big tree by the side of the trail, thrown, and its feet tied securely. Then a man with a big knife made a deep slash in its throat. Blood gushed from the wound and the buffalo struggled hard against the men who were holding its head down. To us it seemed needlessly cruel and the "tough guys" of our party who were standing by for the kill, myself among them, watched with mingled feelings, to say the least. When the animal had bled to death, the work of skinning and cutting out the meat began and here J.P. was as good as his word, working side by side with the native butchers. The meet looked like good solid beef and, now that the blood letting was over, made our mouths water.

Meanwhile, plans to put us on the move were being completed. It was decided that we would make our start in the morning for Berat. It was one of Albania's larger cities. The place was controlled and had been made into a district headquarters by the patriots. There we would be able to meet high officials and perhaps contact the British agent. Messengers would be sent ahead with word of our coming and arrangements would be made at villages along the way where we would need to stop. The "big man" said the mules would be on hand and ready for us.

It was after five o'clock and we had had no food since breakfast when Hassan finally told us the feast was ready. We trooped back into our room, glad to get out the cold drizzle that had kept us in goose-flesh and clammy clothing all day. We threw some sticks on the embers in the tiny stone fireplace, and waited, with the patience of a pack of ravening wolves, for the food.

We didn't know it then, but we were about to get our introduction to the Albanian style of eating. First, a woman came with a round table that stood about six inches off the floor, resting on triangular shaped pieces of wood. The food came next, in a huge kettle, steaming hot, which was placed on the table. Then from the solemn, silent serving woman, we each received a large metal spoon.

"Hey," observed Paul Allen in an awed tone, "what the hell goes on here?"

Hassan appeared in the doorway.

"Eat." he proclaimed, with a hospitable flourish of his arms, "Be sure to fill yourselves. It is hot. It is good. We are all very happy, no?"

He left as quickly as he had come, evidently his own supper was waiting.

"Ladies first," said Thrasher, in a voice that sounded very tired. Suddenly Jim Baggs' high-pitched cracker laugh pealed out.

"Be damned!" he gasped, gusts of hilarity shaking him, "f-f-fall in you poor whites! Soup to nuts! One spoon, one pot, and here we go! Lord, bless this! Rally around. Kneel and dip, keep them elbows in so none gets hit!"

So that was how it went. Taking turns around the kettle, we licked the bottom clean, hollered for more, and this time we got it. We really made it quite a lark. We were so hungry that we enjoyed it down to the last dip. It was stewed beef, thickened with flour and the inevitable corn bread, but it went down, warmed, and filled us.

After dark a party was made up and went down to finish the job of burning the plane. We pulled off the brush camouflage that had hidden the remains of the C53 through the day, and again splashed gasoline over the hulk. This time we built a fire and tossed blazing brads into the ship until small flames began licking up the raw gas. In a matter of seconds, then the C53 was roaring like a blast furnace, lighting up the wooded slopes of the little valley and putting a lurid sheen on the waters of the lake.

We watched her burn in silence, wrapped in our own somber thoughts; questioning the dark, uncertain future that was before us. It had all seemed so plain and easy when we were planning with the patriot leader back at the house. Now, with the black smoke of the C53 rolling into the night sky, there were doubts. Baggs popped a cigarette into his mouth and his lighter made a pin-point of brightness against the gloom that was closing in as the pyre of the ship lowered.

"Well sir," he said softly, "she was a damn good ship and she done all right by us."

He gave the visor of his cap a tug.

"That's that," he announced briskly. "Let's go boys."

4 – Meet Hassan - Patriot Warrior

November 10, 1943 – Wednesday - Morning

What would happen if the Germans caught us? That was a question that came in for quite a lot of talk. We were all in uniform, but our association with the Albanian patriots, whom the Germans classed as guerillas, might affect our chances of being treated as ordinary prisoners of war. Thrasher summed it up.

"If the Jerries get us," he said, "They'll damn well do what they please with us, uniforms or not. We'd better keep out of their way as long as we can."

Back from burning the C53, we were all gathered in our room where we were disposing of the few papers from the plane and those of our own that might identify our unit or contain other bits of information in case we were captured by the Germans. About all we had left were our tags, which gave only our names and army serial numbers. We were all kind of quiet and blue. I dropped into the fire a letter I'd written my mother; one I'd planned to mail after reaching Bari. It looked as if the secretary of war would be doing my writing for me. Lebo had spent part of the day tinkering with the radio, but reported that a vital part of it was gone. So that was out. And the compass from the plane was also no good.

On the brighter side, the rain had stopped and, as we watched the British have another go at the German air field, the star speckled sky overhead gave promise of clear weather. We spent another uncomfortable night, dozing and restless in the crowded room. Up and out early, we watched the rising sun burn the white mist from the mountains, and eagerly waited the start for Berat. The mules the Albanian leader had promised us began to arrive shortly after daylight, each one attended by its Albanian owner. They were scrawny, small, and unkempt, but we were to learn that they were tough as hickory, could carry remarkable loads, and were sure footed, mountain wise animals. Each carried one of the crude wooden saddles and when the loading began we found that every mule was to carry a load of baggage with space left for a rider. The Albanian drivers treated them as they would a hoe or a shovel, except for feeding. There was none of the bond of comradeship and kindly understanding that is so often the case between men and horses or other stock in America. The Albanian mule, placid, lazy, perfectly gentle (those we saw), seemed to be simply a piece of equipment that, unfortunately, was alive and had to be fed. To see one of them with the saddle removed, day or night, usually meant the beast had reached the limit of its endurance and was about to die. The Albanians did not mistreat their animals deliberately; they merely used them without mercy or sentiment.

We hustled along our preparations while the rising sun warmed and began to dry our damp clothing. We tore two chutes from the plane into strips, which we used for scarves. Allen saved the cords, saying he'd promised to bring some to his girl.

"If you get back," somebody suggested.

"And if you still got a girl," another added. Paul only grinned at them.

Baggs was showing one of the Albanian soldiers a Mae West jacket. He helped the man into it and quietly tripped the inflating valve. You could almost see that soldier's hair pushing his hat right up on his head as he felt the jacket filling out. His eyes got big. For a moment he stood as if frozen. Then, suddenly exploding into action, he tore the jacket off and flung it on the ground. Everybody, including the Albanians had a big laugh out of it. Baggs saw the solider was angry, so he showed him the trick with another of the jackets and then let him inflate on one of the rubber life rafts. These and other things that were useless to us, we left at the farm. Hassan assured us they would be put into a storehouse.

"You can get them when your soldiers come to Albania," he said, with complete seriousness. With Hassan, as with many others, it appeared only a question of time before American armies would be fighting side-by-side with the patriots to rid Albania of the Nazis and Italians, although towards the latter a more or less open truce was now maintained.

The day warmed up rapidly and the nurses shed their big G.I. coats, putting some of them, with our two blankets, into padding for the saddle in which Shumway was to ride. Just before our march got under way, we brought the crew chief out and set him on the mule. Some of the girls decided to ride, perched sidewise in the framework of the saddles. Hassan was again mounted on his small white horse, but the rest of us were setting out on foot. We soon found that we could make better time that way, easily keeping ahead of the mule train. It was pleasant, moving along the wooded side of the mountain that morning, although still plenty wet under foot. The scene that slowly unfolded before us was one of rugged beauty, the deep green forested folds of the hills lying silent and without a sign of civilization for as far as we could see. We would have had to remind ourselves that there was a war and that we were deep in enemy territory if we had wanted to keep our situation clearly before us. But for most, spirits had soared, and we moved along the trail as if we were a picnic party setting off for a jaunt in the Muskegon River Valley back home in Michigan. Wolf, Hayes, Allen, and I were talking about the day we had rented some saddle horses at Bowman field and had roamed around the countryside.

Suddenly Hassan, who was riding at the head of the column, wheeled and began to wave his arms and shout. He came bouncing down the trail at a trot, motioning vigorously for us to get into the woods. Then, over us, we could hear the hum of a plane. A minute or so later we were able to spot the ship, quite high and small against the clear blue of the sky.

"German," said Hassan. "In good weather they are always looking around."

"What about the rest?" Thrasher asked. "Think they got the mules under cover?"

Hassan nodded.

"My men know what to do," he declared. "We see the Germans; the Germans do not see us."

"You can make it a hundred per cent for us," Thrasher agreed. "We don't even want to see any Germans."

"You must always see the Germans if they are there," Hassan assured him solemnly. "You don't --- pooff! Never mind too bad!"

His eyes and the way he spoke sent a little chill along my spine and gave me a sinking feeling in the pit of my stomach. There was a war all right, and we were in it. The sound of the reconnaissance plane was fading into the distance.

"Now we go on," said Hassan calmly, and led us back to the trail.

At one o'clock we arrived at a small mountain village where the party was divided into two groups for the noon meal. It was corn bread, but Hassan explained that because these people considered it an honor to serve American soldiers there would be some turkey. We each had a small piece. It was stewed. We saw almost no broiled, baked or roasted meat in Albania, except the little we cooked for ourselves.

"Reminds me of our own little Orville," Owen mused, as we munched our turkey. "We have to get back in time for Thanksgiving."

"Little Orville" was a small Sicilian turkey, purchased in partnership by Owen and our mess sergeant to be fattened for our

Thanksgiving feast. They named him Orville, they said, because with a name like that it would be easy to kill him.

It was three o'clock by the time we got under way again and after about an hour we came out on the banks of a very swift river, the first we had encountered and typical of Albanian streams, cold, fast-running, fairly deep water. We asked Hassan if it was all right to drink and, getting his nod, we dropped down on the bank and had our fill. Hassan and all the Albanians we met were amazed at our capacity for water. "Enough for horses," they said. Most of the men waded through the stream, but the nurses shuttled across on the mules. This took quite a little time as it was nearly dark when we all assembled on the other side. There Hassan told us that we were now very close to the Germans and that we must proceed as quietly as possible, "no smoking or talking," he said, "and keep close together."

After about an hour of darkness we came into another small village, making our halt at the house of the council president or political leader. Arrangements had been made for us and, in groups; we were taken to various houses for the night. Hassan and his assistant, a man we came to know as "Acorns," came with the group I was in. Our supper was corn bread and rice, served Albanian style, every man for himself and the devil taking the hindmost. Or so we thought. Hassan corrected us gently.

"Always," he said, "a little is left in the pot for the ones who cook."

Paul Allen halted his spoon in mid-air.

"Cripes!" he exclaimed, "this is all they got, huh? Lay off, you birds! You want these people to call us a bunch of hogs?"

This comment from Allen, whose 19 year old appetite had already won him top rating as trencherman of the outfit. We tore him to bits.

"OK, OK," he grumbled, red faced, "but imagine that. Sticking their whole damn meal out in front of us and taking what's left. Why they wouldn't even do that in Kentucky!"

The lower story of this house was a cattle barn and the family lived on the second floor. We had what appeared to be a store room. There was a mattress on the floor on which four of us were to sleep. We put one side of it against the wall and on the other side we moved up a tombstone that was in the garret, to give us a little more width and keep the outside man from rolling off onto the floor. Zieber was on the outside and claimed he spent the night on the tombstone to keep from being kicked black and blue by Allen. Hassan read us the inscription on the stone and said it would be used for the grave of the man of the house when he died. Oh, no, he wasn't sick; it was just a common thing for a man who prospered to provide himself with a stone for his grave.

"A pleasant custom," observed Hayes. "I bet a guy could make himself a mint with lighting rods in this country. Work them right together, see? First you give them the works on protecting life and home with the rods. Then if it's no soap, you simply flip the catalogue over to tombstones. Get it? If the guy won't buy rods he ----------."

"Sure," interrupted Zieber, "good as dead. Boy, you got something there. Let's you and me come over here after duration and rake in the dough!"

"What is this dough you rake?" inquired Hassan politely, and we all roared.

"Oh, so ----- money," he said, when we had explained. "That is very easy never mind."

He bummed one of my fast dwindling stock of cigarettes and then, settling back against the wheat bin, where he and Acorns had spread their blankets on the grain, launched into a tale of brigandry, a regular children's hour thriller, with all the parts acted out, keeping us spellbound for an hour. We had thought that stage coach hold up men were figures of the long past, but here we were talking to one who was at his prime and at the peak of his career. Of course it was the war. I don't believe Hassan would have been in such work in peace times. He operated as a patriot and he made the Barley's pay plenty, a Robin Hood in the Balkans.

We asked him how he had gained his place as commandant of the band that had picked us up and he said that was also a very simple matter. He would be commandant, he explained, as long as he killed more Germans than anyone else in his particular district. This was also a business developed to the point of routine. Hassan and his hill men lurked along roads used by German patrols, contriving various schemes for getting the Nazis to stop and leave their vehicles. When the ruse succeeded, then half-dozen rifles would spit from the brush and the Germans would drop. When Hassan and his party succeeded in killing off the entire patrol they would wait for darkness and then go down and pick up what they wanted, sometimes even making off with the car. At other times they would watch the German air fields, hoping for an Allied raid. Then, amid the dim of anti-aircraft fire, bursting bombs and rattling machine guns; they'd lay out in the brush and pump lead at every Nazi they could catch in their sights.

We looked at this man, our friend, of whom we had been thinking as somewhat of the comic opera character. No older than some of us, he was a veteran killer; his life at stake in almost every move he made and death, sudden and violent, the price for a slip on a single detail. He worked full-time at war, a grim, dirty business, in which he accepted the odds of being in his own "backyard" as against the best that modern military might be able to muster, a game in which the only rule was never to give the other fellow a chance. We began to find our friend Hassan not so funny.

November 11, 1943, Thursday – 11:00 a.m.

On the Trail to Berat

In the morning we assembled and pushed on towards Berat, moving in much the same fashion as we had the previous day until about 11 o'clock when Hassan halted us. At this point, he said, we would leave the train and get over behind a ridge which would furnish us cover while we passed a German air field in the valley, below and ahead of us. This meant rougher and slower going, but before we had gone very far, Hassan took us up the slope to a place from which we could see the field, not over a mile away. He seemed interested in the field, using a pair of field glasses (German, I suppose) to scrutinize it carefully. We definitely did not like this neighborhood and waited, with some impatience, while Hassan made his calm survey of the enemy drone. What he was looking for, if anything in particular, we never learned. There were a number of planes in sight on the ground, but none took off or landed while we watched. At last Hassan lowered his glasses, restored them to the leather case, and then, without a word, led us back to where our mules and their drivers were waiting.

Twenty six years ago on this day and hour the guns of the First World War fell silent along the battle lines in France. We spoke of it being Armistice Day, recalling memories of it in the past, although for practically all of us that first Armistice Days was a much a part of history as the first Fourth of July. Lt. Helen Porter, a nurse from Hanksville, Utah, told of visiting a fortune teller before we sailed from New York. The crystal gazer told Porter that she would be in Berlin before the year was out. That guess, right now, was reaching too far in the realm of probability to be a joke. Then somebody suggested that the glass might have been misread slightly, that instead of Berlin the woman should have said Berat. We agreed the mistake was natural because who had ever heard of this Berat. Lt. Porter said she had no inclination towards seeing Berlin in 1943 and wouldn't be too disappointed if she never were there.

We continued behind the ridge until about two o'clock when we halted again.

"This is now a place where there are some times Germans," Hassan told us soberly. "It is only an open place here they would see if they are out but to go around makes closer to them. I put my men to watch from both sides. If the Germans come, do not run. You go one and then one, here. If it is only one or two Germans, maybe three, we kill them and you go on quickly --- but after they are dead. You are sure of that first. If more than three ---," he shrugged and spread his hands, "I am sorry. But I do not think it so."

It was awfully quiet in the woods. We avoided one another's eyes. This was it. Thrasher spoke first.

"Got to cross here, huh? No other way?"

Hassan shook his head. Then he laughed reassuringly.

"This is not a bad place," he said. "It is only that you know what to do. I do not think we see any Germans here, no, no, no, --- but -----," he shrugged again. "Now," he said, "I go with my men."

We waited while he placed his soldiers. During that few minutes our two officers and the nurses removed their air corps wing badges and their bars of rank. Hassan came back.

Now," he said, "I take the first one."

Baggs stepped forward.

"I'll be seeing you," he grinned. We watched him out of sight along the slope of the mountain as he followed Hassan. We waited in tense silence for the sharp snap of a rifle in the woods ahead. But none came and in a short time our guide returned.

"So easy never mind," he smiled.

It really turned out that way. When my turn came I went off through the woods with Hassan. In two minutes we were at the edge of the clearing, pausing a moment to listen. Then Hassan gave me my instructions.

"You must walk from the woods to the woods," he said. "You are just out picking flowers and looking at birds, no? You go to that big tree --- you see? --- all the others are small." He told me that Acorns would be waiting to meet me. "Go now," he said, quietly, "we are watching."

It was open, natural prairie, a distance of perhaps 400 yards at the point where we crossed. The difficult thing for us, of course, was not to hurry and not to take cover. It was quite like the openings one comes on in the Michigan woods, country I'd been at home since boyhood. But I did not feel much at home right then. I think that if I'd caught sight of a moving object anywhere in the length of that prairie, I wouldn't have been "picking flowers," I'd have been picking them up and laying them down, taking it on the lam, getting out of there pronto. But all was quiet and when I got to the big tree there was Acorns, grinning broadly. You couldn't be sure about these damned Albanians. They made you think you were in a tight spot and then, when it as all over, left you wondering if it wasn't just a little joke they'd cooked up to amuse themselves. But we had to take them at their word because we didn't know anything. Maybe German patrols did pass through that clearing. Signs showed that somebody had been there and not too long ago either. But we didn't wait around to see if any of the Jerries came along that day.

Hassan now led us along a narrow, upward trail, cautioning us to be quiet. He said we were within easy range of enemy small arms fire, but here again we don't know because we weren't fired on. Before so very long, we entered a small village and it was decided to spend the night there since our crossing of the clearing had taken a lot of time. Berat, we were told, was four hours away. That's the way they always measure distance in Albania. Distances in miles would be deceptive. They divided us again into groups. We had a hearty meal of corn bread mashed in sour milk and served Albanian style. Then we settled down for the night. Just before we dozed off, Hayes nudged me.

"Orville," he said, "I been figuring. Only about ninety hours ago we were sleeping in our bunks back at Catania. Boy! I used to think that was a hell of place. But --- it'd sure seem like home to me now. Isn't that funny?"

"Funny as a busted leg," I grunted.

"Yeah," Hayes signed, and that was the last I heard.

We were strung out on the trail, a straggling line of nurses, soldiers, Albanian patriots, and plodding mules, haphazardly mixed when in the depths of the slightly overcast sky next morning there was the deep, far off rumble of engines. Earlier in the day we had seen an airfield deep in the valley and some distance ahead. Near me now, an Albanian was slapping his mule, urging the little beast to shelter under a large tree. I didn't know it then but a tree affords some protection from falling pieces of flak and spent machine gun bullets. I got under the tree too, while the sound of engines grew louder. Hassan arrived riding back along the trail.

"The English pay the Germans another little visit," he said, showing his teeth in a wide grin as he passed us.

Suddenly the planes whipped into sight.

"British hell," I heard Shumway shout from a short distance away. "They're B-25 Mitchells!"

Sure enough, those twin engine bombers blazed the big white star of the American air force from their sleek slides. The pound of anti-aircraft guns filled the valley below us with the surly clamor of war and ahead of the Mitchells the sky began to bloom with bursts of flak. The bombers roared directly overhead as they closed on their target. We were out on the trail, going crazy with joy at the sight of American planes. We swung and waved everything we had at them, parachute panels, coats, musette bags, anything we could get our hands on. We threw our flight hats into the air. We were yelling like Indians, abandoning ourselves to wild enthusiasm, forgetting that Hassan's order for the day was to stay under cover. Tears of joy ran down our cheeks as we watched those big ships sweep in for the kill. Two German fighter planes rose above the tree tops and made circles around the field, but we paid no heed to them. We heard the mighty thumbs as the bombs struck the Nazi drome. One bomb overshot and burst with a great upheaval of flames and smoke on the hillside opposite us. A thick column of black smoke began reaching into the sky from the direction of the field. The flak was furious now, but the two Nazi fighters stayed downstairs, offering no opposition whatever. They were taken up only to escape destruction on the ground. In the space of minutes it was all over, our planes ducked out of sight beyond the shoulder of a mountain. None of them had been badly hit so far as we could tell, but one was spitting a plume of dark smoke and seemed to be dropping slightly behind the formation.

There was no hint that they had seen us. Pilots and crews were intent on their mission and even if our mad celebration had been noticed, they were too high and too swift to have recognized us as Americans. Yet it was the topic of conversation for the next hour as we plodded along the trail. What if the miracle had happened, that they had seen and recognized us and would report us back at HQ? It could not make much difference in our situation, but, as one of the nurses suggested it might slow up the routine of sending the messages to our folks. That was a hope we all shared. I venture there was not one of us but who had thought of those telegrams going into our homes. I'd thought of Mom sitting there in our little house there on the hill with the yellow paper in her lap and maybe my picture on the table --- "regret to inform you that your son Sgt. Lawrence Orville Abbott ---."

"I reckon they'll go slowly anyway," Baggs predicted. "A transport crew's liable to show up after being missing a month. It's happened before and we aim to make it happen again."

So, it was on to Berat and that British agent. We didn't know how he'd be able to help us, but we had been given the impression that once we contacted him our troubles would be over. We were all taking turns on the mules now. That is, there were usually empty saddles somewhere along the line and if anyone felt like riding he simply waited until one of the empties came along and hopped aboard. We usually rode side saddle with our feet dangling over the wooden slats. The mules were so docile and knew the trail so well that they needed no attention. Three of us, Wolf, Allen and I, were riding in such fashion that afternoon when a little bit of "mule-play" went on between the animal that Wolf was riding and the one Thrasher straddled just ahead. On Thrasher's mule, the little oat bag that hung somewhere on every one of the saddles, was being carried on a rear peg where it dangles temptingly before the eyes of Wolf's mule. Wolf notices his steed edging closer to Thrasher and, as a little widening of the trail gave him opportunity, he slipped quietly forward, thrust out his scrawny neck and deftly lifted the oat bag from Thrasher's saddle. Allen leaped to the ground and started forward.

"Give it to him," he muttered, "be damn if that ain't rich!"

But the owner of Thrasher's mule had seen the theft and hustled back to recover his property. Paul was ready to fight right there, but we grabbed him and hustled him away. Thrasher, meanwhile, had ridden on, oblivious of the whole incident.

November 12, 1943, Friday – 10:30 a.m. - Entering Berat

We were pushing along through the woods, just as we had been for the past two days, when suddenly the trail broke over the edge of a high bluff and there in the forested valley below us lay a small city which we knew must be Berat. Some of the party was already working down over the trail that angled along the steep hillside.

Berat was divided by a river that curved out of sight behind a fold in the hills a short distance below the town. Most of the buildings were low, one or two-story affairs, and all seemed to be of white stone or stucco. Along the hills, back from the river, were several ranges of terraces with houses built on them. Tall white spires lifted from a number of structures which we took to be churches, and there were winding white walls everywhere. It looked like a very old town, like a picture from our history books. Yet, though it was strange and quite unlike anything I'd ever seen, the river, the valley and the city brought me a quick mind's eye glimpse of the old Muskegon and Newaygo, my home.

We descended to a road that followed the course of the river, coming out on the highway near the walled gateway to the town. People began gathering around us almost at once, shouting strange words and smiling. As we entered the city it became evident that news of our coming had been spread because the street we were on quickly became jammed with a singing, shouting throng. The word "Americano" rose again and again, people hugged us, tried to kiss us. Our progress was slow and we had trouble keeping together. They were singing the song we later learned was the Albanian national anthem, and then at other times we would hear a tune we recognized as the "Star Spangled Banner." Here and there, people were shooting their cameras at us and one fellow evidently made a business of it because on the following day there was a whole window filled with our pictures in a shop in the main street.

We were tired and hungry; we couldn't see what all the fuss was about until word got around among us that we were being welcomed as invasion troops, the boys who were going to drive the hated Germans out of Albania. And Thrasher, carrying the Tommy-gun from the plane, had the only piece of armament we owned. Soon a large building loomed before us and in front of it we at last came to a halt. Allen pushed his flight hat far back on his head and eyed the place dubiously.

"Boy," he exclaimed, "this doesn't look too good, but I sure hope this is where we eat!"

Standing beside him, Jim Cruise let his musette slip to the ground.

"Strikes me," he observed, "that these folks are going to be pretty damn disappointed when they find out we're nothing but a bunch of pill rollers."

5 – Escaping the First German Raid

November 12, 1943, Friday - Berat

Paul didn't get his wish for food. The building housed the patriot headquarters. We were ordered to bring in our baggage and told it would be stored there under patriot guard. Hornsby came in and dumped his barracks bag to the floor.

"All I got to say," He announced gloomily, "I hope these guys haven't been talking to any marines. If they have, we're kissing this stuff goodbye right now. They'll strip us. Them marines ----."

"Shut up," somebody hissed, "don't you see the high pow-pow is giving us a speech?"

"Can't eat words," Allen grumbled.

But Hassan, acting as interpreter for the patriot official, soon explained that we had been invited to dinner at the city hotel and we gave the big boss a cheer. Out we marched and down the crowded street to another building where we were ushered into a large, well furnished room.

"Fellas," said Sgt. Allen in a low tone to a group of us gathered in a corner, "If they bring another bucket of that corn bread slum after this build up, I'm going to start busting windows. And don't any of you birds hold me back!"

Pretty soon a woman came in with a tray filled with little cups. She went first to the officers, including the nurses and then to us. In the cups was a small quantity of an almost colorless liquid. When all had been served, the big chief and another man who had accompanied us to the hotel, made a sweep with their cups that took in the whole party and then downed their drinks.

"Well," said Owen, "I don't know what it is, but ------."

We drained the cups. Allen grunted so that he could be heard all over the room and then drew a noisy breath. My eyes smarted and I could feel that liquor burning its way down my gullet.

"White lightning," was Baggs' sotto comment.

It was our first experience with raki, the Albanian national drink. In about fifteen minutes, during which we stood around wondering what was going to happen, the serving woman came in with another tray of cups. Allen took his, looked in it, then rolled his eyes to the ceiling and sighed loudly. This was coffee. It was jet black, very sweet, and almost as thick and smooth as syrup. We liked it, and followed the example of our host by taking it in little sips.

"Well," Hayes ventured, "seems as though all this swank ought to lead us to something pretty good."

It did. It was a real nice meal with a couple of slick male waiters doing the serving in the big dining room. There was mutton, potatoes, gravy, and a whole apple for each of us, the first food we'd enjoy in five days. There was plenty to eat, plenty to drink, and dishes to eat from. This was more like it.

At the close of the dinner we were told that a new man, one we came to know as Kostig Steffa, was to take charge of our party. Lt. Thrasher sent for our Tommy-gun and ammunition and asked that Hassan be called in. Hassan tramped into the room, marching stiffly in his big rubber boots, and obviously embarrassed by the fine surroundings and the show of rank at this table. Thrasher got up and shook hands with him, thanking him, in English, for what he had done for us. Then he gave Hassan the gun and the clips of cartridges.

"Good-bye, Hassan, and good luck," our pilot said.

Hassan stood at attention, his eyes meeting Thrasher's. "To you a safe journey," he said in his precise accents. Then he added, "Tungjatjeta---I may see you again."

We watched Hassan stalk out of the room; Hassan, who had come to us there in the rain and mud, and who had guided us over the hills to this haven. Hassan, who told us he was so very glad to have someone, besides the birds and the trees, who he could talk the English. Hassan and his "never mind." Hassan, who killed Germans like we kill pheasants back in Michigan; we had said good-bye to a friend.

After dinner we loafed around the hotel talking to some of the people who could converse in English and then were taken back to the council house where we were given a few Albanian cigarettes and received our assignments to billets. In groups of two or three we were introduced to the people who were taking us for the night. After that, we were more or less split up, some being shown the city, some of the men being taken to barber shops where their hosts treated them to shaves and haircuts. The man I was with and several others took a few of us to an Albanian bar not far from the hotel. The bartender, who also owned the shop, was a man named Chris, a heavy set fellow with a small black mustache and dark hair that was thinning on top. He had spent some time in the eastern part of the United States and talked almost like an American. The man who took our orders said something to him as he reached the bar.

For Christ's sake!" roared Chris, "They are Americans! They can have all they want and there's more in the cellar!"

After a while Chris came over to our tables. He wore a couple of flannel shirts covered by a blue pull-over sweater, and had on leather lined britches and black leather puttees. Thinking of Hassan's boots we suspected that part of his garb was of German or Italian origin.

"Business is good," he declared genially. "I sell plenty and have plenty for myself." He laughed. "But I don't like this GD war," he concluded.

Chris made us as royal a welcome as he knew how. He plied us with drinks and then insisted that we come to his house for supper and spend the evening there. So we had more good food, some good wine, plenty of tobacco and cigarettes, and with Chris and other Albanians who had been in the United States, we made it quite like an old-timer's reunion. We told them all we could about America and they told us many things about Albania.

November 13, 1943, Saturday 09:00 a.m. - Council of Berat

That night we had a real sleep, the first since we'd left Catania. In the morning we had to be routed out to make our nine o'clock date at the council house and for some of us, whose heads were heavy from the large evening with Chris and his cronies, it really took some routing. I would have been well satisfied if they had let me sleep the clock around. Just to be in a bed was luxury in the ultimate.

At the council house we were formally introduced to a man named Gino. He was said to be the highest ranking officer of the patriots in that area. Gino was in what I guessed to be an Italian officer's uniform. He had an Italian Tommy-gun and a pistol in a black leather holster was hung from his wide leather belt. After the preliminaries, we were seated, and Gino began to talk to us in Albanian, stopping every few sentences to let our man, Steffa, put the stuff into English for us. He was giving the history of Albania, beginning with the cave men as near as I could make out, and the lecture lasted three hours. Gino evidently hoped we would carry a good part of the story home with us. But I doubt if any of us got enough out of the translation to do much along that line.

"This guy talks like we're going to live here," muttered Cruise, who was seated beside me.

That was really the point. We had no interest in staying in Albania. Our whole interest was in getting out of Albania. But out of the ordeal we did get some information we wanted. First we learned that the British agent was not in Berat. Then we learned that the town was practically under siege by the Germans and was being defended by the patriots. Our fate appeared to be inevitably cast with these fighting mountain men of the poorer class, although here in Berat there was also the Balli Kombetars, or Barleys we come to call them, who were mostly the rich and well-to-do people. Between the two fractions there was friction of a sort, the patriots often accusing the Barleys of collaboration with the Nazis. But the differences had not yet led to an open break and hostilities between them.

When the lecture was over we were again taken to the hotel for dinner. Thrasher was made banker for our party. We all turned in what American money we had and, through Steffa, I suppose, he was able to get it changed in Albanian Napoleons. That afternoon we attended several meetings around town, drinking toasts, having more pictures taken, and being generally feted by the citizens. In the evening we went to a theatre where we saw a motion picture of some of the fighting between Italian and Greek troops on the mountains of Southern Albania, little realizing that before we left the country we would be on foot in those very mountains. After the show we were assigned to homes for the night.

November 14, 1943, Sunday – late morning - Berat

On Sunday we rose late and some attended church, which pleased the Albanian hosts very much. Just before dinner we assembled at the council house and were taken, in a group, to visit a castle situated well up on the hill and overlooking the city. On the way back we visited a hospital and the patriot barracks and guardhouse where four German prisoners were being held. We also visited a well kept cemetery. Greek graves were on one side of the road and Italian on the other. Many of the graves were those of Italian flyers who had been shot down. They had pieces of propellers or other parts of the plane inserted in the stones. On other graves, under a small glass, would be a picture of the corpse.

On our way up and down the streets, the Albanian natives insisted on greeting us with that closed fist salute and "Vedeke Fashisme." We got so bored with it finally that, although we agreed with the sentiment, most of the boys descended to a mumbled "ah, to hell with you," accompanied by a loose wave of our right arm. Wine flowed freely again at dinner that day and among the enlisted men there were at least some "borderline cases" before we got through. In the evening we again went to the theatre, seeing a musical show done by young Albanian players. The seats in this place were just loose wooden benches. Steffa explained that the star of the show, a dark haired handsome youth, had been in Rome as a student when

Mussolini began his invasion of Albania. The boy had given up his studies to come and fight Italians and had remained to fight the Nazis.

J. P. Wolf and I were quartered together that night. It had been another big day for us. The bed felt very good, and for a few minutes we lay there in the dark, talking over events and casting up the sum of our chances, pro and con. We were on the optimistic side. We had been comfortably housed, well fed, and were among friendly, hospitable people. We had been assured that the British would be notified of our presence and the plan seemed to be to stay in Berat until arrangements could be made to get us through to the coast.

"And as far as that goes, Orville," J.P. declared, with a hearty yawn, "they can leave us right here for the duration without making me too sore."

"We could do worse," I agreed.

Then we went to sleep.

November 15, 1943, Monday – 05:30 a.m.

Germans Attack Berat

Grey half-light was in the room when a violent shaking of the covers around my shoulders roused me.

"Uh-huh," I grunted, "OK."

The agitation stopped and I went back to sleep. But the man came again, shaking me and muttering something about Germans and patriots.

"Po, po, po," I replied drowsily, burrowing back into the covers. Outside there was a vague sort of tumult that gradually beat its way into my consciousness. Sounded something like rifle and machine gun fire. I could feel J.P. stirring, and rose up on my elbows to listen.

"What do you make of it, soldier?" I asked. "Think we should get up?"

Johnny opened his eyes and stretched his arms above his head.

"Patriots and Barleys are having a little ruckus maybe."

Just then we heard what sounded like a bracket of heavy stuff thumping into town. We both swung our feet out onto the floor. More shells broke and the fire seemed to be creeping closer to the house where we were. Wolf stood up.

"Do you remember Hassan telling us the Barleys don't have any artillery?" he asked.

"You're damn right," I answered, making a jump for my clothes. "Those shells have got 'made in Germany' on them!"

Our teeth chattered and we shook all over, not entirely from the clammy chill of the room. Our host came rushing in again while we dressed.

"Quick!" he yelped, grabbing me by the arm. "Germans! Guerro Patriots! Germans! They come! Run! Run!"

Johnny and I tumbled out into the street. People were shouting, waving their arms, running in every direction. Overhead, now, there was the roar of war planes and we observed a flight of four Nazi drive bombers circling the city. A column of Patriot soldiers came down the street on the double, scattering civilians before them like a flock of squawking chickens.

While Wolf and I stood there, trying to make up our minds which way to run, Cruise, Owen, Hayes, and Zieber came along at a dogtrot.

"Fourth of July in Technicolor," grinned Hayes.

At the moment it seemed that Jerry was using ack-ack, since the sky overhead was filled with the puffs of bursting shells. But as we watched, we saw that incendiaries were being mixed with it.

"Give me a cigarette, Orville," Jim Cruise begged, times are getting tough."

"You're telling me," I muttered as a shell exploded about thirty yards down the street from us.

"Goodbye boys," said Zieber, "I'm shoving off, right now!"

"Roger," agreed Wolf and handed Owens the butt of the cigarette he had been smoking. I joined Zieber and Wolf, but the other three stopped to put on their leggings. The chatter of rifle and machine gun fire could be plainly heard from outside the city somewhere. We trotted along, weaving our way through the excited people of Berat. They were moving out, using everything on wheels they could push or pull, vehicles piled high with bed clothes, clocks, chairs, pots and pans, crocks, bulging bags of all sizes. Some were able only to save what they could pack on their backs. There were old men and old women, struggling with heavy loads, tears streaming down from their faces. Mothers moved along with babies in their arms and squalling children clinging to their skirts. Not many we saw had been hurt but plenty of houses were shot up and I guess none of us who were in Berat that day will need another lesson on the text "War is hell," even though what we saw was hardly more than a border skirmish.

After leaving the boys at our billet, we didn't pick up anybody from our party. In the commotion and excitement we hardly gave a thought to where we wanted to go. All we knew or felt at the moment was that we were like the people of Berat. We were losing our "happy home."

6 – The Germans Advance in Tanks

November 15, 1943, Monday – Leaving Berat

J. P., Zierer and I were three pretty uncomfortable American lads right then. We hoped that we could find our way back to the council house, but we didn't know whether we'd find any of our gang when we got there. Could they have been pulled out; while fighting off our Albanian host, we were trying to go back to sleep? There was no question in our minds but that the city of Berat was doomed. A half dozen German fighter bombers were over head, covering the uproar on the ground with the savage, relentless snarl of their engines. In every street people were rushing into and out of the houses; the streets themselves presented scenes of wild commotion; and in the background was the noise of the battle, drawing closer as the Nazi panzers drove towards the city gates. Again and again, as we moved along, we encountered those trotting columns of Albanian fighters, grim faced mountain men, among them boys younger than we, sometimes women soldiers, all armed, all moving steadily towards the fighting front. But this was no Indian fight. The full fury of modern was hitting Berat that morning.

Coming towards us down the street was a middle aged woman, bare footed, walking rapidly, her face a blank as far as emotion went, her eyes glassy, staring. Over one arm she had a jumbled mass of clothing and in her other hand was a glass pitcher. There were whole families being led by gaunt, grim grandmas, mothers with bawling infants in their arms; young boys and girls staggering along under the burden of their younger brothers and sisters.

"Let's join the Partisans and get in this GD fight!" yelled Zieber; voicing a thought I also had been rolling around in a mind that seemed to be emptied of everything but the sights and sounds around me. But we kept on going and suddenly I heard J.P. shouting,

"Come on, Orville! Shake it up! I see some O.D.!"

We were in sight of the council house and there were three or four trucks lined up in front of it with people milling around them. We put on all the speed we could, dodging, weaving and sliding through the flow of refugees. As we drew near we could see nurses and soldiers in the trucks, among the civilians. Breathless we swarmed aboard one of the vehicles after jamming our way through the crowd. Boy! It sure was good to be back with the gang.

The truck we were on gave a lurch and began to move slowly ahead, squawking its horn to part the streams of civilians. Soon after we started, Sgt. Bob Owen came up riding a horse he had picked up and with him were Cruise and Hayes, who clambered aboard the truck. We were all carried away with the excitement, everyone talking and shouting without thought or memory; swaying and struggling to keep our feet as the vehicle, an Italian army cast off, rumbled along towards the outskirts of the city. Some of the gang decided to walk and had little trouble keeping the truck in sight, as slow as its progress. But at last we cleared the town and were out into open country on a narrow gravel road, full of ruts and dips, which made an old truck wallow like a boat in a heavy cross swell.

Hardly had we gone half a mile when the vehicle jammed to a sudden stop and the driver leaped out, throwing his arms up towards the sky and shouting "Boom!---Boom!" We poured out of the truck and scattered in all directions, seeking cover. Owen dismounted and tried to drag the horse off the road, but the animal balked, tore loose, and then loped away with Owen in hot pursuit, followed by Allen, who was just running to be away from there. Zieber leaped for a ditch and safety. He was safe, but the ditch was filled about three feet deep with water and sewage. I knew nothing of that until later, because I was doing a fast sprint down the road. After what was probably the best 100 I ever ran, and knowing I'd pass out if I went much farther at that rate, I ducked off into the brush. Pounding foot steps were close behind Horsby and Wolf plunged into the cover with me. For a minute the three of us stood there, our faces turned up to the planes that had alarmed our driver. We figured they were dive bombers, but it was obvious that their target was the town rather than our trucks. As we watched, a machine gun opened fire from off of our left. The gun was in the ruins of a burned out hospital building, and the line of the tracers coming from the emplacement showed us that the Nazi pilots up there had little to worry about. Looking towards Berat from the slightest elevation we had attained, we could see smoke that appeared to mark the battle line, and other columns of smoke that looked like burning buildings.

Many of our gang got back on the truck, but J.P., Hornsby and I decided to push along on foot for awhile. Some minutes later we heard a car coming up behind us. It was a tiny Fiat, about like one of our Austins, and the driver, an elderly man, obligingly halted as he came up with us. We rode the fenders of the little machine for about three miles. Then, ahead, we saw three men in American uniforms plodding down the road at a dog trot. We motioned the old chap to stop the car. It was Lt. Thrasher and SSgt's. Eldridge and Ebers, and we joined up with them. We continued along the road until the tuck overtook us and then clambered aboard.

In less than a minute the truck stopped and our driver again took to the woods, leaving a trail of wild yells as he went. We hit the dirt and once more dove into the brush. This time it was an observation plane, floating high overhead and paying no attention to us. We were ready to kill that driver with our bare hands, especially Shumway, who was able to get around, but none too nimble on his lame leg. We walked back to the truck with profane grumblings. While we were getting loaded again the truck ahead of us started up just as an Italian soldier got one. The man went sprawling on his back in the road, his rifle on top of him. Allen and Hornsby helped him back to our truck and shoved him up among us, his helmet knocked to a drunken angle and his eyes still rolling from the shock of the fall. Hornsby then picked up the gun and got aboard as our old truck wheezed into motion again.

With clattering motor, whining exhaust, and grinding gears we rolled slowly along until we came to a wide curve where our driver once more went into a boom fit and set off for his mountain home. It was no false alarm. Two ME 109's swooped out of the blue and did a riveting job on the truck as they circled at a low attitude. I scrambled up a wooded hillside and found a cave entrance, protected by an overhand of rock. Wolf and Lt. Anne Markowitz followed. It was Markie's birthday and J.P. still gasping for breath, took the opportunity to wish her "many happy returns." Markie managed a smile and said the only "happy return" she wanted was to New York. Meanwhile, the Nazi fighters disappeared as swiftly as they had come. But the stabbing spurts of flame from those guns; the thwack and whine of bullets splattering from metal parts of the truck, had cooled any enthusiasm I had for riding. Wolf and Lt. Markowitz decided they'd do some walking too. So we set out, keeping the general direction of the road, but taking advantage of small ravines and gullies for cover. Any plane was an enemy plane. Jerry had no air opposition whatever.

After we'd gone a little way, we came out near the road and saw Lts. Kanable and Dawson and Sgt. Cranson and Cpl. Hornsby. By this time, the truck was out of sight ahead of us but that didn't worry us because Lt. Thrasher had told us he'd been directed to a village farther along this road and we assumed that by keeping on it we'd be certain to rejoin the party. We crossed a small river and just behind it came to a woods road that led sharply up grade towards a small building that looked like a chapel. We stayed on the gravel for a bit and then, when we saw a chance to save some distance by cutting across a bend, we took to the brush again. Down in the center of the bend we could see two trucks halted, with a crowd of people standing around them, but decided that neither of them belonged to us. As we came out on the road, we sighted our truck a few yards away, stopped, and the passengers making for cover.

Several German fighters were closing in on the vehicle. They did a thorough job, weaving back and forth across the road at tree top height, spitting .50 calibers. On their first run, Shumway, who was in a shallow ditch only a few feet from the truck, had his face showered with gravel and dirt from the bullets. While the planes swung out and turned, our crew chief got up and hobbled about 30 yards to a spot less hot. Then the Nazis roared back over, cutting loose with everything they had. Four times they went over, slamming their concentrated fire into our old truck and as much of the road as they could reach. We pushed ourselves into the dirt of ditches and ravines, cursing them with a rage made doubly hot by the knowledge that we were helpless. Paul Allen was so mad that he popped up after each run to shout at the Nazis, jumping up and down like a three year old in a tantrum.

"You dirty, lousy, ----- ---- so-and so's," he bawled, "One P-38 could knock the lot of you kicking'!" Down he went into his ditch. Then up again. "You'll get yours!" he bellowed at the tails of the Nazis, "And all I hope is I'm there to see it!"

"Hell," he said, with a sheepish grin, "now where are we going from here?" Then he looked down at something he held in his hand. It was a .50 caliber bullet, still hot against his palm, a little souvenir that didn't quite give him the Purple Heart.

None of us knew where we were going; all of us knew we had to keep going. So we started out, a couple of the nurses and four of us enlisted men. The Albanians who had been on the truck had scattered and we saw no more of them. Shumway limped along with us, "old step-n-a-half," he called himself, and told us to go on ahead but to leave some marks for him to follow. We told him we'd stick together; we seemed to be ahead of the main part of our group anyway. Pretty soon we rounded another bend and there was a horse, nibbling grass at the edge of the gravel. It looked like the beast that had given Owen the slip when we first piled out of the truck, but whether or not, we lost no time capturing it, since it made no effort go get away, and put Shumway aboard. About two miles farther on, we came to a small outpost of Italian soldiers. We couldn't understand them and they couldn't understand us, except for one word, "American." But by signs they made us know we were to go with them. Right then we weren't sure whether we even wanted to understand the sign language.

"This could be bad," J.P. said, "damned if I like it. We ought to stay on this road and keep moving."

"Oh, they seem friendly enough," Markie observed, but her tone was a little anxious. We all looked at the swarthy soldiers in their greenish, belted coats and odd shaped steel helmets.

"Guess there isn't any argument," Shumway suggested, "those guns are loaded, you know."

We set off with our guides or captors, whoever they were, and soon reached an Italian machine gun nest in a pass between two mountains at a point well above and overlooking the road we'd been on. There was an officer with several more men here. The leader, who could put out and understand a little English, set our fears at rest. We were with friends. Then he barged off into Italian, making quite a long speech, gesturing, and darting his eyes now and then towards the horse. We didn't get it at all. But after he was through, one of his men led the animal away.

"One up and one down," commented Shumway, with a shrug. "Hope they don't hang horse thieves around here."

The horse probably belonged to the Italians or they might have known who owned it. Perhaps they were just confiscating a horse. We were in no position to object. The officer gave us some Italian anchovies, army issue, and since it was past noon and food hadn't been on our list that day, we sat down and made what meal we could of them. By that time we were thinking that this was a good place to wait for the rest of the gang, anyway.

Beyond the horizon there was still an intermittent mutter of gunfire and mingled with it in the valley before us was the faint rumble of a motor. As we finished our food, two Albanians appeared on the road, walking rapidly. They turned off and made their way up the gun post. It was our friend Steffa, from Berat, and his right hand man, Mohamet. We gave them a hearty welcome, but Steffa cut it short with a wave of his hand.

"The Germans are on the road with tanks," he said, "it is not safe here for you. We must go on very fast."

Even as he was speaking we saw two of our nurses and two enlisted men break out into the road below us and start running. Wolf waved his arms and yelled at them. They came on up as quickly as they could, making us a party of four nurses and six enlisted men. The exhaust sound of a motor in the valley grew louder. Steffa ordered us all out of sight.

"Go behind," he snapped, "get down! Do not let them see you!"

He and Mohamet suited action to the words and we all took cover. The four girls were in a little hollow, behind the knoll on which the machine gun was set. Down on the road the roar of a motor grew suddenly blatant and a German tank waddled slowly into sight around the bend. It came on, while we watched from our concealed positions, moving to the foot of the ascent to the pass. There it swung sharply across the road and stopped, it's motor purring at idling speed.

Not a German left the tank. The hatch was not opened. The machine simply sat there in the road, a mobile pillbox. Perhaps Nazi eyes within its steel walls were searching our position carefully. Perhaps they had merely stopped to have a smoke. We'll never know about that. But we spent a pretty breathless ten minutes, waiting there. Anyway, some of us did. Lt. Kanable was powdering her face, doing a very careful, critical job of it in the little sanctuary back of the gun. There, almost without shifting my eyes, I had a view of an American girl, seated cross legged on the ground, calmly absorbed with her make up before the opened case with the mirror top, while, less than five hundred yards away, a tank full of Nazis were making up their minds what to do.

I'll always think that these were Germans, who had learned to shun too penetrating a curiosity about Albanian hills; who had learned not to go poking about off the main roads, even behind the armor of a tank. At any rate, after a few minutes the tank driver revved up his engine, spun the nose of the big machine back towards Berat and then sent it lumbering back down the road. Steffa hardly let it get out of sight.

"Now," he shouted, clapping his hands, "now we go!"

"But where are the others," asked our nurses, almost in unison.

"Oh, they take another way. We will see them in this village I am taking you to," Steffa answered casually.

We could see that the girls didn't like this idea so well, and we too wanted to be sure we weren't leaving anyone. So we cross examined Steffa as best we could. He seemed to be very sure of everything. Did we remember the side road, right after the river? That was where the rest of the party had gone. They had been waiting in the chapel on the hill. When we did not come, Steffa and Mohamet came to look for us while the rest went on to the village by another way. That was the best we could get and we had to take it.

Steffa led, followed by the nurses, then we six enlisted men, and Mohamet at the end of the little column, as we took the mountain trail, winding steadily upwards through good cover. J.P. was carrying the rifle belonging to Steffa, but Mohamet packed his own plus an Italian pistol in a leather holster.

It was a quiet party. We were down to bed rock, and I suppose we all knew it. Stripped of most of our supplies, which at best were small; split off from the rest of our people; our hope of contacting the British gone; and not knowing at what moment we might find ourselves trapped by the Nazis, our outlook was anything but promising. All about us now were the strange, still woodlands, soaked with the fall rains, the grey sky overhead giving promise of more moisture, the wind on our faces sharply cool and burdened with the dank smell of wet leaf mold. Behind us, the sound of the day long battle for Berat was almost gone. No need to ask or doubt the outcome. The Germans had guns, tanks, and planes. Berat would be in the Nazi grip before dark. For us there was no going back, whatever the future might hold.

"Give me a cigarette, Orville."

Paul Allen's voice broke in upon my somber thoughts.

"Fresh out," I answered, and told the truth.

"Yeah," he muttered gloomily, "And I'll bet Hornsby's bag back there in the town hall is furnishing the Jerries good American smoking right now."

"Hope they bust a few teeth on those dog biscuits of mine," I added.

The bulk of the stuff we had salvaged from the plane was gone. Those of us who had our musettes had some medicines, here and there a package of K-rations, a few odds and ends, most of which were now the common property of all of us, not to be used except in case of necessity.

November 15, 1943, Monday – 3:00 p.m.
Mountain Village Outside Berat

At about three o'clock we came into a little mountain village where we met a tall, elderly and very dignified Italian colonel whom Steffa seemed to know. They carried on a brief conversation in Italian. Steffa could speak Italian, Greek, English and I think German. The colonel called one of his soldiers and sent him hustling off on some kind errand. He then shook hands very formally with each of us. We were then led to a small church and went inside to rest while Steffa did some interpreting for us.

"He says he is very glad to see the Americans," Steffa told us, "but knows nothing of the rest of your people. He thinks all the

Germans have gone to the battle at Berat. But it will be better for us to go farther to the mountains. This is not the village your people are coming to. We will see them in the next village. It is about two hours from here. Our friend," Steffa shifted his eyes to the colonel, "and his soldiers will help us make this journey."

We spent about twenty minutes in the small, dusky room of the church. An Italian soldier brought in food, some wheat bread, the first we had seen, aside from the holy bread at the churches, more anchovies, and for each of us, an egg. These supplies the colonel himself passed to us. I put my egg in my pocket, hoping it wouldn't get broken before I had a chance to cook it. J.P. did the same with his. We ate the bread and anchovies and then went outside where we found a group of Italian soldiers with a mule on which they had loaded Shumway and our few items of baggage.

That was a rugged mountain trail, steep, very steep in spots, rock strewn, and tortuous. It was slow going and hard work. A good thing we had the mule for Shumway. That knee of his had about all it could take for one day. We kept at it, struggling and puffing over the bad spots, the girls doing about as well as any of us, everybody giving his companions a hand whenever he was in a spot to do so and it was needed. Steffa, Mohamet and the Italians, used to such work, were taking it easy, but for us – it was a long way from flying transport. Two hours passed and we were still toiling along the trail. But around 5:30 p.m., as dusk was falling, we entered another village.

Steffa took us to the council president and after being received by him we were assigned to quarters. The nurses were put in one house, the enlisted men in another, and the Italians in a third. Dinner was served Albanian style. We were back on cornbread and cheese, this time varied by some nuts. We took the food and were glad to get it. After the meal tobacco became our most important problem. We all joined in the chorus of "I'm Rolling My Last Cigarette." Wolf had a large size Duke's Mixture bag and I made a deal with him to fill it if he'd roll cigarettes for me. He agreed and I went out on the quest, not too hopefully. But I ran into some natives and was able to work a trade for some home grown stuff they had. Wolf and I rubbed it up for cigarettes, seated in front of the fireplace in our billet. It was plenty stout, but it was smoking. Better than nothing. Steffa was with us and gave us quite a lot of news as we loafed about the fire, talking over the eventful day.

He thought the Barleys were to blame for the attack on Berat; that they had called the Nazis in. When we pressed him for the reason he said it was probably because of the argument between the military and the town political leader. The military wanted a wholesale execution of the Barleys and the civilian authority was opposed to it. The Barleys, evidently getting wind of how things stood, concluded not to wait to see which faction would win. Steffa also told us that the Nazis would have our pictures, those shots taken when we marched to Berat and later displayed in several store windows. We asked what difference that would make.

"For you, bad --- if they catch you," he said. Then he smiled. "But they don't catch you yet."

"What do you mean --- yet," I asked bluntly.

Steffa drew out his large white pocket handkerchief, shook it with several sweeps of his arm and then blew his nose.

"In war," he said, gazing at the fire, "you do not ever know." His eyes turned to me suddenly. "You remember last night----the boy who sang ---the young hero of what you call – opera?"

"My God," I said, "was that only last night?"

Steffa fixed his eyes on the fire again.

"Dead," he announced calmly. "Last night he sings, he is beautiful, he is strange, free, and happy. Today there is a shell -- some rags and blood. War."

All right, All right. We knew the score. We had to trust this Steffa. But I was thinking of that slick little game Hassan told us about. Money was so easy. Oh, the chap was saving our lives. It would be his neck as well as ours if the Nazis got us. But ... would it?

7 – Three Missing Nurses

November 16, 1943, Tuesday – morning

To the Village of Matishave

Our gang was up early Tuesday morning. We slept in our clothes, and it seemed as if we had spent most of the night trying to get warm and in a comfortable position.

"Never slept a wink," declared Allen, "not a damn wink the whole night."

"Hell," growled Hornsby, "you were snoring five minutes after you hit the floor!"

"It's a lie," yelled Paul, "I never closed an eye hardly all night and I don't snore!"

Hornsby ripped out a derisive oath. "You hear that?" he shouted at us. "O.K. wise guy," he went on icily, "if you were so damn wide awake what time was it Orville got up and went out to ----."

"How the hell do I know," Paul roared back, "you know I haven't got a watch? It must have been around two near as I can figure."

Hornsby turned to me with a sardonic smile.

"Tell him, Orville," he pleaded, "go ahead and tell him."

Of course I hadn't been out at all. But I wasn't taking sides. I told them they both snored and for good measure added that Hornsby talked in his sleep. Steffa stood by, taking in the little exchange without a glimmer of what he thought on that poker face of his. Everybody felt tough, but there was no use yapping about it.

Breakfast was cornbread and rice. Then we all got together at the village square. The village square, in Albania, is merely a small patch of level ground near the center of town which is usually paved with smooth flat stones and used as a threshing floor at harvest time. They pile it full of cut out grain and then drive horses or mules over it to tread the wheat or rye out. We loafed around the square nearly all morning. Steffa told us that there would be word from the other party before noon. We tried to talk to some of the Italian soldiers and Albanian civilians who gathered around, eyeing us curiously while they talked among themselves. Mid way of the morning, a Nazi transport plane sailed by overhead and we took cover.

"Reinforcements," Nurse Rutkowski guessed.

The girls took it all very much as we did. Now and then people would come, bringing small gifts, mostly food to them. One motherly old girl popped a small round corn cake into the hood of one of the nurses' coats as it hung at the back of her neck. It gave them an idea that was useful from then on. The hoods, when not in use, were most apt to be carrying bread, cheese, nuts, or whatever bits of extra food the girls had.

The clouds were breaking up, scudding along the sky in squadrons, and sending moving patches of sunlight across the wooded slopes all around us. The sunshine felt good, although the temperature was not low. Steffa walked about, making the most of his position as leader of our party. I suppose he was telling the people that we were American invasion troops. The patriots simply refused to get that idea out of their heads. I guess it sounded too good to them to give up even though it wasn't true and we told them so many times.

"It is good for our people to see that the Americans are coming," Steffa would say, and smile at us. "When they see the Americans are here, they are happy to go on fighting. I wish I could show all the people in Albania that we have Americans with us."

"And I believe you'd do it," I heard Lt. Gertrude Dawson say softly. It took longer than that for me to get the idea, but it finally did penetrate. Steffa would be taking us up and down Albania like a traveling circus if he had his way. One of the other girls asked about the message from the other party.

"Very soon," he smiled, "po, po, po, yes, yes, very soon."

It was nearly eleven o'clock when the word came in by patriot soldier. It said that the balance of our group was about one hour behind us, this was Steffa doing the telling, and that we were to proceed to the next village about two hours away and farther up the mountain.

"We'll wait for them," said Lt. Dawson quickly, "and all go on together."

Steffa drew his handkerchief, flourished it, and wiped his nose, shook the cloth out again and then replaced it carefully in his pocket.

"That would be foolish, he said, with a smirk, "They do not come by this way."

I believe Dawson was ready for a showdown with Steffa right there. But how the devil could we fight with Steffa? He was the only English speaking native within miles, for all we knew. We had not the slightest idea where we were or where we should go. Our only possible choice would have been to start back down the mountain to meet the other part of our gang. And that would have been more foolish than staying where we were, if, Steffa said, they were not going to this place. We gave it up. We had to go on being performing bears for Steffa. Lt. Anne Markowitz had the last word.

"Steffa," she said, in a friendly tone, "you know we want to meet the British, don't you? You will take us to them?"

Steffa looked out over the valley a moment, then his eyes shifted back, glinting with the smile that lifted the corners of his mouth.

"Yes, yes, yes," he answered, then after a pause, added, "but first we must find out where they are."

"How far it is to Greece?" Hornsby asked suddenly, looking up from licking the cigarette he had just finished rolling.

"You would not wish to go there," Steffa said, spreading his hands. "We have little --- they have nothing. It would be so foolish."

It was like trying to pin down a breeze with a thumb tack. The only thing that remained to be settled was "when do we start?" and Steffa did that by leading the way out of the village. Along the way, Steffa pointed out the mountain battlefields where Greeks and Italians had fought.

"Looks like we might be heading for Greece at that," Sgt. Cranson remarked.

"Hope so," I said.

"Why?" asked Wolf, who was carrying Steffa's gun, "have you got friends there, Orville?"

"No, but they are a great people for barber shops and restaurants; and I'd like to see a few of them."

The trail was upgrade and not easy. Steffa let us string out, setting whatever pace suited us. It seemed evident that he no longer feared contact with the Germans, and this proved correct. We saw the battle grounds of former wars, but nothing to remind us of this one. At about one o'clock we came to a village and again went through the ceremony of meeting the council president and the commander of the small Italian garrison. Quarters were assigned and the Italian gave us another ration of anchovies. About the middle of the afternoon word came that the other party was about three hours behind and would be in the village the next morning.

"What are we trying to do?" one of the boys inquired, "run away from them?"

Supper was served Albanian style, on one of the low tables that we all gathered around. The food was the usual cornbread and cheese.

"Tonight I'd even appreciate you're playing on the mandolin, Orville," Allen declared during the long, dreary evening.

"God help me," agreed Cranson, "so would I. It would be better than drawing a blank, like this. If a man had some cigarettes and a little real food, I could stand it."

We spent another miserable night. We'd been given blankets, one for three of us. It seemed that when Allen didn't snore he kicked, and when Hornsby and I finished trying to stay under the blanket with him, stumbling out into the gray light of the dawn, we were in a murderous mood. But I couldn't stay mad long with that big Kentucky kid.

November 17, 1943, Wednesday morning

This morning I boiled the egg the Italian colonel had given me, and we had some small pancakes for a little variety with our breakfast of cornmeal mush. Carrying the rifle for Steffa paid J.P. no dividend; the butt of the gun smashed his egg flat in his pocket. When he heard it go, Johnny stood there on the trail looking just like a kid who had wet his pants. After breakfast we rolled us some smokes and sat around talking about home and food and the rest of our party. After a while we went down to where the nurses were quartered to see if we could pick up some news. They had it and they didn't like it. It was that our people were now about four hours behind us and would probably be in the village by noon.

The girls gave us a warm welcome and were glad to see us. They had been waiting for us to show up before calling Steffa in for a pow-wow. They didn't believe Steffa had even an inkling of where the rest of our gang was and that he didn't care whether we ever saw them again or not. They wanted to get the truth. If Steffa was lying to us, and we were pretty well agreed that he was, then, for all we knew, the rest of our group might have been captured by the Germans, some might have been hurt or killed. If they were out of the picture, we'd have to make some plans for ourselves instead of just going along expecting to join the main group again. The nurses, holding commissions, were in command of our party. They wanted to talk to Steffa, so Wolf and I went out and rounded him up. Dawson started the parley.

"Steffa," she said, "you told us Monday that our people were one hour behind us; last night they were three hours away; and now it is four hours. Why is that?"

Steffa chuckled low in his throat.

"They are more than we," he said, "it is a longer way – they go more slowly."

"Are any of them hurt?"

"No, no, no, I do not think so."

There was a short silence. Lt. Dawson stared hard at Steffa, and when she spoke again, seemed to have settled some things in her mind.

"Steffa," she began, "we are American soldiers. We can do no good in Albania now. We want to get back to our places in the American army as soon as we can. We are thankful for what you have done for us here in Albania, but we are not going to be your prisoners, and if you keep us here we will have tell our commanders that the Albanians ----."

A ragged fusillade of rifle shots interrupted her. Three Albanian soldiers rushed into the house, jabbering excitedly at Steffa, who snapped a terse sentence back at them. They stampeded for the door, leaving us in a heavy silence. Steffa smiled reassuringly and shrugged.

"A little wedding party," he said, "it is nothing."

Paul Allen rolled his eyes around our circle.

"Must be one of our old Kentucky shotgun hitches," he grinned. "'About the first one I ever heard to reach the shooting stage though."

We all laughed quickly, then our breaths caught as another clatter of gunfire rolled along the mountain.

"You must keep away from the windows," Steffa said quietly, "and we will all sit on the floor."

"They really put out for a wedding, don't they?" Allen drawled. "I'm getting homesick!"

We laughed some more at that and then went on with the wise cracking. But our ears were tuned to what seemed to be a first class skirmish going on outside. Steffa gave us no further enlightenment; however, and in the course of a few minutes the shooting dwindled down and stopped. An Albanian came into the room, spoke to Steffa, and then left. Steffa turned to us.

"He says your friends are in the village below us and your captain says we are to go on to the next place."

"Oh—oh," J.P. exclaimed with deep sarcasm. We looked at the four nurses. Lt. Dawson glared at Steffa. No one spoke for a few seconds. Then Dawson relaxed with a little gesture of despair.

"All right," she said. "Let's go."

November 17, 1943, Wednesday – To The Village of Burgulla

That was a beautiful trip along the mountain. The sun came out bright and warm and, although we traveled at an easy pace, we were soon perspiring. Back at the village we had said good-bye to the Italians and were now being escorted only by Steffa and his small detail of Albanians. Shumway was on foot.

"Hell," commented Allen, "he could have walked all the time."

"Sez you," grunted the crew chief, but grinned.

The Italian colonel made quite a fuss over Markie at the leave taking and gave her a spot of raki that she said was like a ball of fire all the way down. Now and then, along the trail, she'd stop and fan her open mouth with her hand.

"You'll learn not to take drinks from strangers," J.P. joshed her.

About an hour out we discovered a beautiful waterfall that appeared like a white feather some distance away and as we drew nearer to it somebody suggested we ought to stop for showers. The idea, spoken in jest, was developed to a point where some of us almost acted on it, but our experience, with the chill of Albanian streams, finally brought a thumbs down decision. Farther along we sighted puffs of flak far off in the sky and could make out small specks of the aircraft, but never knew whether the ships were American or British as they did not come our way at all. We pulled up in the village at about three o'clock and were taken to a small hospital were we were received by the doctor and his staff of three Albanian nurses.

We had dinner at the hospital, another meal marked by the appearance of some wheat bread. Then there were more anchovies. After dinner we stayed at the hospital for about two hours. The three Albanian girls entertained us by singing some of their native songs. The Albanians like to sing and wherever they were, on the trail, good weather or bad, in the houses, at the village square, they'd be likely to start up a war chant or a song of some kind. Much of it, as here tonight, was without accompanying instruments. Sometimes they'd have a flute or two, very rarely a stringed instrument. We enjoyed resting there at the hospital, listening to the songs the girls sang, though of course we didn't understand the words. They asked us to sing for them.

"I know one," Dawson said. She began to sing the Negro spiritual, "Ain't Gonna Grieve My Lord Any More." We all joined as much as we could. It was a song we were to sing often in the days to come on the Albanian mountain trails. Then we sang other American songs, and it was quite a pleasant evening.

We had been assigned to our billets and just before leaving the hospital word came from Steffa that the other American party had arrived in the village we left that morning and that we would see them about ten o'clock that night.

"But he told us they weren't coming that way," Markie said quickly.

"Two to one they don't show up," Hornsby offered, voicing the doubt this message brought to all of us.

These Albanian villages are strung all along the mountain. As a rule our billets would be separated by a mile or more. The nurses were especially uneasy about the situation, and after talking it over we decided that it would be better if we all stayed in the same house that night, or at least find some quarters that would keep us close together.

Ten o'clock came and went. I was sore. I'd taken Hornsby's two to one in tobacco, and that was serious. We rounded up our friend Steffa. I jumped him first.

"O.K., Steffa," I said, "what's the story now? Its past ten o'clock and they aren't here. We want to know why and we want to know right now."

Steffa shrugged.

"I do not know," he said.

"I believe you," Dawson put in, "and I doubt if you even know where they are. You're going to keep us wandering around these mountains as long as you can."

"Let's take off for Greece in the morning," I suggested, more with the idea of seeing what Steffa would say to that than really intending that we should do it. But the others didn't give the play a chance.

"We've done just as you said, Steffa," Dawson went on, after the heckling had quieted. "We've let you take us from this town to that town, we've trusted you. But now --- we're through! If we have to find our way out by ourselves, we'll do it. We're all through being pushed around. The Barleys are friendly to us and they have ways of getting us out."

"Oh, don't offend him," Nurse Rutkowski pleaded.

"The Barleys will betray you," Steffa declared in a loud voice. "They will betray you just as they do all the others. With them it is only money. Do you have any money?"

He knew of course that we had nothing except the small amounts Thrasher had doled to us at Berat after we pooled our funds.

"Yes," Dawson told him, with her chin up, "we have plenty of money. If necessary we can out bid the Germans or even buy up some of them. You've been telling everybody we are American soldiers. Do you know what that means?"

"Let us be friends now," said Steffa blandly. "We have now a little trouble with the Barleys, but ------."

"We're not your friends," Dawson told him, "we are your prisoners!"

Steffa chuckled softly.

"We do not take prisoners," he answered, "unless they are our friends."

That probably was a fact, but Dawson was determined to make her point.

"Steffa," she said firmly, "we've had nothing but talk for three days. We are going to start getting out of this country and back to where we belong. It may sound crazy to you, but we can do it and we're going unless you're mighty quick about showing us results instead of talk!"

"Tomorrow," said Steffa, with an enigmatic smile.

"All right," I said, "and if the rest of our gang doesn't show up, we're on our own, understand?"

"I understand."

Steffa left us then, without another word. For a moment we stood there in the dim lamplight of the room, listening to the soft crunch of gravel under the feet of the patriot leader in the roadway close to the door. From outside then came a short, low murmur of voices as Steffa spoke to one of his men. Then silence. Paul Allen explored his shirt pocket for the cigarette that wasn't there, shook his head absently, and sighed.

"Well, said Hornsby briskly, "anybody want to bet we don't see them tomorrow?"

I took him, double or nothing.

"You and your big mouth, Orville," Paul said, with pitying sarcasm. "There isn't that much tobacco in the country!"

Dawson hadn't moved from her place near the lamp table.

"I've got a hunch they'll be here," she said, smiling.

Out in the street we took stock of our papers and making and rolled us some smokes. Three Albanian sentries were in sight from where we stood. Overhead a bright round moon was playing hide and seek with dark wisps of cloud. We didn't talk much, but what little there was indicated that our thoughts were running over the line of action we could take in case the rest of the party didn't come in. After a few minutes we walked on down to the billet Steffa had shown us, and in spite of the doubtful future, had a fair night's sleep.

November 18, 1943, Thursday Morning

On Our way to Dobrusha

Breakfast next morning was highlighted by white bread and some honey and an egg for each of us. After the meal we went over to the hospital, where the nurses spent the night, and found them getting ready to go to a small stream nearby where they planned to wash some clothes and do some bathing. When we asked them for the morning communiqué they told us that Steffa has stopped with word that the other gang would join us by noon.

"I think this time he means it," Dawson said.

"And I just hope he does," added Markie.

They wanted to wait until noon before doing anything or even making any plans, and of course we agreed. We spent part of the morning on a wash day expedition too, but the bathing was sketchy to say the least because the water and air were plenty cold. While we were at the stream rifle shots began popping back towards town. We were glad of an excuse to finish with that icy water and hustle back to the village. When we got there we found that the shooting was merely a few of our patriots sharpening their marksmanship on targets.

The hours passed. Noon finally struck but we saw nothing of the twenty missing people we wanted so badly to see. We made up our minds then to leave Steffa and his Albanians, provided we didn't find out we were, in fact, their prisoners, and push on south through the mountains toward the Grecian border. Somewhere along that line we hoped we might stumble onto one of the many small parties of British operating in the mountains. Steffa took our announcement of this decision quietly and made no effort to detain us.

"It is late in the day to start," he observed, "could you not wait until morning?"

Oh, the fellow had the whip hand. But we were just enough fed up with his stories to be ready to go through with our plans regardless of all obstacles. While we waited we laid out a scheme in which four of us enlisted men would fan out singly form the town and see what we could turn up, leaving the nurses and a couple of men here for a base. If we found anything that looked like a gain, the whole party would then move on to that point and from there we'd repeat the process.

While we were building this house of cards, Steffa came to us beaming.

"There," he said, making gestures towards the shoulder of a mountain. "They come! Look!"

Following his directions we could see a column of people moving up there, but they were too far away for us to tell whether they were Americans. Steffa said it would take about an hour for them to reach the town. We stopped talking about going to Greece and kept our eyes fixed until they hurt on that little column moving slowly down the mountain side. Sometimes there were hidden by the forest, at other times they were in plain view. But before thirty minutes had passed we knew they were Americans, our gang was coming in.

November 18, 1943, Thursday –3:00 p.m.
807th Reunited at Dobrusha

We gave them a joyous welcome, literally with open arms, as they came straggling into town, led by a patriot named Johnnie (*to differentiate from John P Wolf sometimes called Johnny).

"We brought the retreating army with us," Thrasher said, with a wave of his arm back towards the hills."

"Save me a butt on that, brother," piped the voice of Jim Cruise, "times are really tough."

We all made one happy mob, moving down the roadway to the hospital. There we crowded into a room and filled the place with chatter and laugher until suddenly a girl's voice broke above the babble, high and excited.

Where's Porter?"

The hubbub died quickly into silence, broke almost at once by Thrasher's voice.

"My God, isn't she with you?"

"And where's Lytle and Maness?" somebody yelped.

Silence came again. Then Baggs spoke.

"Who saw them last and where?" he asked.

More silence. Each of us thought back over the way out of Berat. Nobody spoke. In the commotion of leaving no one had thought to make a check, and at the time, it would have been of little use. We had all been jumbled with Albanians in several trucks and were hardly more than started with the first plan alarm had scattered us. From that point to this there had never been a time when we were all assembled so that a check could have been made. We faced the truth slowly. Not one of us had seen any of the three missing nurses since we left Berat. They were back there somewhere, Lt. Helen Porter, a Utah girl, Lt. Ann Maness of Texas, and Lt. Wilma Lytle from Kentucky. They might be in German hands, maybe hurt, perhaps seriously, in the bombardment of the town. It all came back, the bursting of shells and bombs, the chatter of guns from the Nazi fighters; the uproar and confusion; smoke, flames; and in the midst of it, three American girls.

8 – We Have Dysentery

November 18, 1943, Thursday - Dobrusha

Thrasher sat with his head in his hands. Baggs stood looking out of a window, his back turned to the room. Nobody said anything for a minute or more. I stole a glance at Wolf, wondering if he was thinking about our meeting with Thrasher on the road out of Berat and wondering why he'd be in such a rush to take off before he knew whether any of the rest of us was getting out. The natives, perhaps, stampeded him the same as they had us; waking you out of a sound sleep by yelling "Run! Run! The Germans are here!" I guess it never occurred to anybody to call the roll as we left Berat. It came to me; too, that C.B. was a flyer, not a line officer, and that affair back in Berat was no "wedding celebration." The voice of one of the nurses broke the silence.

"What are we going to do about it?" she asked quietly.

"I'll go back!"

"Me too."

"I'll go."

A number of the enlisted group quickly volunteered to go back to Berat. Thrasher looked up. He stared at us for a long moment. Baggs swung around from the window. I thought then that I wouldn't be in Thrasher's place for twice my back pay. The pilot stood up, his slim figure sagged with weariness, the leather flying jacket hanging open and loose.

"Nobody goes back," he said, slowly, "from now on we're sticking together."

"Let me take a couple boys, C.B.," Baggs pleaded, "and see what we can do."

"Listen," Thrasher said, speaking as if he was pulling each word up from a fifty foot well, "you wouldn't even know which way to start without a patriot or two to guide you. If you did get back to Berat, you'd run smack into the Nazis and probably find there was nothing you could do."

"But are we going to just go as if we didn't care what happens to them?" one of the girls broke in.

Thrasher turned his head toward her.

"We've got to go on." He said, "Don't you realize that? People in these little mountain villages can't manage to feed a party like this by the week. Besides that," he went on grimly, "it isn't a case of what happens to them. It's already happened. They either got away or they didn't. If they didn't, we can't help them; if they did make it, they're as well or better off than they'd be with us."

Dawson surprised me then.

"Where's Steffa?" she asked.

Steffa came in. The news he had was that the Germans had taken Berat, but he added that he did not expect them to hold it for very long. They'd probably loot the place of food and other supplies they could use or wanted and then retreat as they did in the smaller places. He told us that the nurses, unless they had accidentally been captured, would be with the Albanians who would help them.

Dawson moved over to him. She held out her hand, and when Steffa did not respond, reached down and took hold of his right hand, covering it with her left.

"Steffa," she said, laying it on the thick, "I'm very sorry we didn't trust you and made you so much trouble. You'll forgive us, won't you?"

"Po, po," said Steffa, without much enthusiasm.

"It would be so easy," Dawson went on, "for you to find out about our friends for us. Don't you think you could have your men find them and bring them back to us?"

Steffa pulled his hand away slowly.

"I would do anything," he said gallantly. He flourished his handkerchief and blew his nose loudly. "But it is not possible," he added, tamping the cloth back into his pocket. "I do not have the men to go and the people of Berat are in a thousand places. It would take much time. It is not possible," he repeated. "No, no, no!"

Dawson held him with her eyes.

"Please try," she urged softly. Steffa sighed loudly.

"I will try," he promised, and turning to Thrasher said gruffly, "do you want to buy a goat?"

"Hell yes!" Thrasher exploded, startled by the swift change. "We're hungry. We'll buy a whole damned buffalo!"

"Do not have buffalo," Steffa commented dryly.

Pay him, C.B.," J.P. urged, "then just lead me to that goat."

The spirits of the party lifted noticeably. We were getting things straight in our minds. The toughest break we'd had so far had put us down for the count, but we were coming back. Everybody began talking; we went over the whole thing again from start to finish, and arrived at the same conclusion. Much as we'd have liked to do it. We couldn't stage a march on Berat and rescue those three girls. All we could do was to hope that they were among friends.

"Porter and her fortune teller," Nurse Tacina mused. "It was Berat or – will it really be Berlin?"

The group who had been with Johnnie had a story of their own to tell. They had been caught in a feud between the patriots and Barleys and at one time were nearly surrounded by Barley riflemen who were carrying on a lively skirmish with the patriots. But Johnnie had managed to get them clear of the battle zone by traveling long hours at night and over rough terrain. It was the first time, they were told, that the smoldering distrust and dislike between the two factions had broken into the bright flame of open conflict.

Quarters were arranged for the night, the nurses staying at the hospital and the rest of us assigned to a house "a little way down the mountain." It took us an hour to get there. We sat around the place talking on the inexhaustible subjects of home, food and methods of escape. We also had our mouths made up for a fine supper of goat stew. Then J.P. came in. He walked over to the fire and spread his hands to the warmth, his hunting knife sheathed snugly at his belt. We all fell silent waiting for a bulletin from Wolf on the status of the stew. Finally Paul Allen couldn't wait any longer.

"You bring out meat, Wolf?" he asked. Johnny turned from the fire and cast his eyes toward the ceiling.

"Nope," he said.

"Why not," Thrasher asked sharply. "We're hungry enough to eat the hide, hair and all."

"That's about what we'll get," J.P. declared. "I ain't even sure the hide will be left."

"O.K., O.K.," Thrasher grumbled, "cut out the comedy stuff and give us the score, can you?"

"You asked for it, sir," J.P. answered. "That goat wouldn't make much more a meal for Joe Stalin's pet parrot, provided he's got a parrot and it isn't very hungry."

"I'll kill that Steffa," Thrasher yelled, his face red.

"He'll be so sorry," Adams told him mockingly, "he didn't know the goat was poor, but it is the war and now we go on to the next place!"

"And be no place when we get there," Lebo added.

We dined on cornbread and rice. We were hungry. It was food. Hell! The people we stayed with brought us some blankets and we turned in only to find that our bed clothes were lousy and full of fleas. We made a night of it as best we could.

November 19, 1943, Friday – Morning: To Derhezha

In the morning we were told there was no breakfast for us since our host was very poor and had given us all the food he had on hand the night before. Lousy, flea bitten and hungry again, we set out for the hospital. On the way we picked up what food we could, every man pretty much for himself. Lt. Thrasher gave each of us a little money for this purpose. At the hospital the girls were quick to tell us that we hadn't missed much by going without the goat meat. Thrasher and Steffa went into a conference and the rest of us drifted down to the village square to await the outcome. At nine o'clock our two leaders appeared. Everybody was to turn in what K and D rations they had and then we were setting out for another village, about two hours away. At this village, it appeared we would wait for the British agent.

Before we pulled out, Thrasher sat down and wrote a note to the British, telling of our plight and asking for assistance. The note was to be carried by one of Steffa's men and might take a week or a month before it was delivered. But it seemed our only chance. Those of us who had been with Steffa still had doubts about the man even having instructions to deliver it. Cruise, who often took a dark purple view of things like this, summed it up when he said,

"We got a walking tour of Albania for the duration," he predicted. "You watch."

Steffa gave his rifle to one of his patriot soldiers and dismissed the small band, retaining only Mohamet and Johnnie to go along with us, besides himself. We also left the Italians at this place. Many of our party did not wait for these final details, but began stringing out of town over a trail that dipped down, moved sharply upward, and twisted hither and yon as only an Albanian mountain trail can do. Part of the time we were sweating, and then at other times a brisk little mountain wind would strike a piercing chill through our damp clothing. We stopped often to rest and let the lagging ones catch up. At one of these points our two guides set a small rock on a boulder about 75 yards away and began shooting at it. Paul Allen watched the proceedings and, when several shots failed to dislodge the stone, made signs to the men to let him try. Mohamet grinned and passed his rifle to the Kentuckian. Paul brought the gun to his shoulders a couple times to get the feel of it, then steadied it on the mark and fired. With the report of the gun the stone whipped off the boulder. The Albanians were visibly impressed, and wanted Allen to shoot some more, but he refused.

"This isn't a squirrel gun," he remarked, rejoining our group. "Say," He went on, "Isn't it funny we don't see any game up here? I don't see signs of a rabbit, hardly any birds, not even a squirrel. I don't even see any tracks or signs. Looks like good game country too. Why if we were down in Kentucky or over in Tennessee in country like this we'd be living off the fat of the land and not worrying if we ever got out, as long as we had ammunition. Come to think of it, I don't believe these people even do any fishing. Streams are cold enough for trout, too."

"Shut up!" I yelled, "Before I bust down and cry. You ought to be in Michigan on the Muskegon this time of year! We'd have us a spike buck easy as you shooting that rock. And fish? Just a couple, fat juicy rainbow, eight, ten pound apiece sizzling over a fire for supper! Owwwwoooo! I want to go home!"

We sat there, each one trying to conjure up an imaginary meal in his home section; Owen bragging the Catskills and MacKinon talking about the Rockies. America was that rich, fabulous, far off place, "just one jump on this side of heaven," Lt. Watson said.

"And can you imagine," Hornsby mused in wonderment, "I used to gripe when Ma put out corn beef and cabbage." He scratched vigorously at a flea bite. "Corn beef and cabbage," he repeated reverently. "Any you birds care for a little corn beef and cabbage?"

"Just enough to stick my head right in the bowl and eat my way out before I drew a breath," said Adams.

"We got the corn," Allen said dourly, "but it isn't beef."

"I'll even settle for some of Brock's Spam has," Zieber suggested.

At one o'clock we hit the village and went through the usual formalities. The trail had been wild and rugged. Swinging along it Zieber, who had been singing snatches of songs in his good baritone, stopped in the middle of a number.

"Why GD," he observed staring around the horizon," there isn't a house in sight anywhere's and I haven't seen one for an hour."

"Just around the corner," MacKinnon assured him.

It was farther than that. About an hour out a cold rain started and by the time we reached the billets we were soaked to the skin. But our host gave us a hearty welcome and soon had a good fire blazing on the hearth so that we could dry out our clothes. The food here, much to our surprise, was excellent, including white bread, macaroni and cheese, and some honey. We were fed and warm and our spirits, at low ebb when we came in, revived swiftly. During the evening a couple of Albanian women came in and did some native dances for us.

"A couple more weeks in this country and we'll all be going through them motions," Zieber mused, and we all had a laugh over that.

The rain continued throughout the next day and orders were to stay holed up, which suited us.

November 21, 1943, Sunday - 9:00 a.m. to Leshnija

However, on the following morning, a patriot solider came in with a note from Thrasher, telling us to be ready to push on at nine o'clock. We hated to shove off into the cold and wet again, but we'd been treated so well here that we did not want to impose further on the good people who had taken us in. Soon, from outside, there came a hail from another group, billeted further out than we, and bidding our host good-bye, we joined them. The man of our house gave us a small bag of English walnuts to take along. We went down the trail, picking up others of our party as we went, and finally wound up in a cow shed on the outskirts of the village where we found Steffa and more of the party, waiting. Steffa was impatient to be off. He paced up and down outside the shed while we stood around inside, cracked nuts, and reported on how we had fared at the houses where we had been quartered.

The Albanians were using the "hill-billy" system of rounding up the party and from outside came shouting and yodeling. A half hour passed with no further additions to our group and the patriots began firing rifles as a signal to depart. Steffa stamped in out of the rain, his brow drawn into a black scowl.

"Ah, what numbskulls these Americans are!" he exclaimed wrathfully.

"Says who?" Shumway popped in the tense quiet that came over us. Jim Cruise reached for the bag of nuts Lebo was holding.

"Give me those nuts," he said. "I'm going to see if I can push them down this guy's throat one by one."

Shumway, Allen, and one or two of the others were also moving towards Steffa.

"Halt, you damned fools," yelled Adams. "Skip it! You want to get us shot?"

A look of surprise crossed Steffa's face.

"Did I say something wrong?" he asked in a tone of wonderment.

"Skip it," Adams repeated, "just skip the whole thing. When do we get out of this hole, that's all we want to know?"

Steffa just turned his back and walked out without a word. Allen reached absently into the bag of nuts Cruise was holding.

"Hell," he said, with a crackle of shells from his big paw, "The guy was right at that. We're dummies, thinking C.B. meant nine o'clock when he said nine o'clock. Why'd you guys leave me sleep? I could'a -------."

At this moment one of the goats wandering around the place hauled off and smacked MacKinnon in the seat of the pants, pushing him into a fresh pancake left by the cattle. Mac took one look at his shoes and began to roar for J.P.'s knife.

"Give me that knife, Wolf!" Yelled above our shouts of laughter, "you guys witness self defense and we'll all have stew for dinner. I'm going to bleed me that buzzard sure as God made little apples!"

"Not with my knife you aren't," Johnny said promptly, and ducked away from MacKinnon's lunge.

It was ten when the balance of the party arrived at the cow shed. They claimed they had been waiting for us at another place and we let it go at that, especially since they out ranked us and it also appeared that we had been sitting pretty in a cow barn, with a fire to warm us and some nuts to eat, while they had been standing around the village square in the rain. In a matter of minutes we were strung out over the trail in our usual fashion.

This day the diarrhea hit us, making it necessary to stop frequently for side trips into the brush. The upset, in many cases developed into dysentery and plagued us more or less from that time on. Most of us joined in placing the blame on our cornbread diet, but it was probably our weakened condition from exposure, fatigue, and sketchy food, more than any one thing. Nearly everybody had it and it slowed us up plenty, but we struggled on through to the next village of Leshnija at 1 o'clock.

Here we were greeted by the president of the council and his staff. We were getting used to the routine of these arrivals, always attended with some ceremony. The Albanians loved it. For us it was in most cases a chore to be gotten through with before we could settle down. At this place the conference of leaders came to the conclusion that accommodations for the night could not possibly be supplied, although it was agreed that we could be fed in groups of four to half a dozen. Word was passed to assemble at the square at three o'clock, after we had eaten. This order was carried out and we pushed on, wearily, towards the next place, which our vanguard reached about five o'clock, the last of the stragglers coming in about forty five minutes later.

We found a priest in charge here. We were assigned to homes and some tobacco was furnished and distributed among the men and nurses. This smoking was welcome, as our fingers and lips were seared from getting the last vestige out of every cigarette. The only small pipe we had was kept hot from dawn to dark, when we had tobacco to fill it. Allen was among the last to arrive in this village, having been forced to make a number of stops along the way. He sprawled on a stone block outside the priest's door and shook his head dejectedly.

"Honest," he declared, "I'm about to wear the buttons off my pants. My belly just growls and grumbles like a couple tom cats making up to fight and yipe! I have got to hit the bushes. Keeps on like this I'm going to measure how far it is by my bush trips instead of by hours. It isn't the time or the distance, fellas, it's the ----."

He stopped as the two pilots, nurses, and several of the men who had been inside talking to the priest came out. We got our assignments. Allen, Owen, Cruise, Wolf, Hayes and I drew together and heard that our billet was "a little way."

"I'll bet it is two jumps in the brush for me if it's a step," Paul assured me darkly. Owen agreed and Hayes cussed.

A rumor spread among us that were to have some horses going on from here. We were skeptical of this news, but Allen took a gastronomical view that held a note of optimism.

"Some horse meat might be a good thing," he propounded as we set off for our lodging. "This damn goat meat doesn't set well with me; it must be too close to mutton or something. Everything we get is soup, cheese or milk; and all of it is mush. And we're getting too much of this damn corn. I've been thinking all afternoon if I could lay my hand on a couple nice cans of pork and beans, oh, mama! Clear me right up!"

"The hell it would," hooted Cruise, "that would be first degree murder! Alas, poor Allen, I knew him well," he declaimed mockingly.

"All right," Paul yelled, "if you know so much about what the," he stopped suddenly,"excuse me, boys," and rushed off the trail, fumbling at his belt buckle.

"That's one," I called after him, "we're almost there, aren't we?"

"Maybe tomorrow we'll find you a German beer garden" Cruise shouted. No reply came from Paul.

"I'm with you on that," Wolf sighed.

Arriving at the billet, supper was the first order of business and in due time it was served, Albanian style. We rallied around the lightly steaming pot of food, knowing it was goat soup thickened with corn bread. Allen stirred listlessly with his spoon.

"Honest," he declared, "this stuff just doesn't do well on my stomach. As soon as I get it down it starts to fizz, boil and then----."

Owen straightened quickly. "Will you kindly shut up and eat your supper?" he inquired icily. He then added, "If we have to hear about how your insides work, you can save it for a bedtime story."

"All right, all right," Sighed Allen in an injured tone, "only ------- --."

"Shut up," yelled Cruise, Wolf and I in chorus. Paul began to ply his spoon in gloomy silence. I'll take oath he dipped twice to our once.

"Those poor girls," he mused, midway of the meal, "it's really -- ------."

Owen choked but again J.P. Cruise and I were in full voice.

He poised his spoon. "All I hope" he went on with a dreamy grin, "is that it hits Adams about midnight and he's up in a loft with a ladder to go down and one of these Albanian blood hounds jumps onto him just as gets the door open. If he gets the door open," he added as a happy after thought.

What'll you have for dessert, Orville?" Cruise asked in sprightly accents, "will a triple-dip chocolate dope do, or could you maybe put away a banana split along with it?"

"Give me a good butt on that cigarette, that's all," I told him. "Hell, I've had enough cornbread and goat soup!"

November 22, 1943, Monday – Early Morning
To Terlioria via Mt. Tomorrit

The next morning we had orders to assemble at the council house. But since breakfast was put out at various times in the billets, those of us who arrived early waited around with the new guide that had been assigned to us. We took one look at his moustache and started calling him "Handlebars." Handlebars joined us because this village marked the limit of territory known to Steffa as his boys, though Steffa and the others were to continue with us. Needless to say there was no sign of any horseflesh, either on the hoof or for the pot. The new guide got a big kick out of being our headman, and when we met Albanians on the trail he stopped to hold long conversations with them, evidently explaining our situation and the part he was taking in it.

Our ailment dogged us. Hayes had a pocket size detective story book we had all read, and he was now called on to make common property of the book so that its pages could be used on our trips to bushes. Toilet paper was not among our supplies. We plodded through to the next town where it was decided to remain for dinner and then push on.

It was just days away from Thanksgiving Day at home. We sat around, rolling cigarettes and passing the little black pipe, talking some, but mostly thinking about the big, fat browning birds in American ovens, pumpkin pies on the shelf, and all the other things that go with the harvest feast.

"Well," said Lebo, flipping a quarter-inch butt into a nearby mud puddle, "we got things to be thankful for."

"Name one," growled Kentuckian Bill Eldridge, looking up from inspection of the sole of his right shoe which was beginning to crack.

Memory is short. When our C53 lunged into the mud by the lake with thirty of us alive and no bones fractured, we called ourselves the luckiest fools in the world. But the present has a way of blotting out the past, and luck, somebody explained, to be really good, must hold. It seemed just then that ours wasn't holding too well.

"I took this flight to get in some flying time," Shumway grumbled. He sighed. "Sure am building it up."

Dinner finally arrived and didn't give us much lift. At the place where I ate it was cornbread, sour goat milk, and onion pie. By the time we were all fed and back again at our meeting place, Thrasher decided it was too late to try to go further. The route immediately ahead would take us over the highest ground in Albania.

9 – Climbing Mt. Tomorrit

November 23, 1943, Tuesday – Mount Tomorrit

Shrouded by fog, the great dark shoulder of the mountain loomed above and before us next morning as we pushed off in small groups for the climb. There were patches of wet snow in the woods on either side of the trail and as we ascended they became more frequent, shooting white tongues out over our path and sending a cold, wet chill through our badly worn shoe leather. It was uphill work, but we were used to that. From time to time the groups would drop out for a rest and a smoke, while others, who were behind, caught up and passed on. Higher up, snow covered the trail, and for the first time since our landing it was all around us.

At a small, level table of land beside a small mountain brook, the party I was with found quite a number of the gang resting and among them was the Albanian guide, who had been keeping at the head of our column. It had been decided that we would all assemble at this place, then keep close intervals and travel as a single party when we started on. The boys were lively, some engaged in a snowball fight. Others were at the stream, filling their canteens with the clear, ice-cold water. And some, like me, were doing a vigorous job of stirring up their lice and fleas. Gradually the rest of the bunch came in and with one of these later groups were two Albanians, who, with our guide, went into conference with our officers. In a few minutes, C.B. called us together.

"Somebody has got too hot on a hunt for souvenirs," he said, giving our dilapidated section of enlisted men a look that was supposed to be grim and stern. "These two men have come after a certain stone. They say this stone is very old and very powerful. It was taken at the village where we stayed night before last. They want it back, so whoever picked it up can shower down right now. It's supposed to be big medicine and plenty bad luck if we keep it."

Nobody spoke or moved for a bit. Our eyes remained fixed on the Albanians flanking Thrasher. They stared solemnly back at us.

"What stone?" Shumway said, breaking the silence, "they can have this whole pile of rocks if they want it."

J.P. shied a snowball at Markie, going rigid the moment it left his hand.

"Cut the comedy," Thrasher urged.

"O.K. chief," we heard Bill Eldridge say suddenly, "I guess this is it." Hell I didn't think it amounted to anything. If it's really hot stuff, they can have it back and welcome."

The stone he held in his hand was a flat, circular-shaped piece with carved indentations around the edge, making it look rather like a crude cogwheel.

"Thanks, Bill" Thrasher said with a cool smile, "these guys claim the bird that took it is going to die anyway, but maybe it'll lift the bad luck off the rest of us."

Bill laughed.

"Don't claim to live forever," he said.

The tension eased as suddenly as it had fallen, and we were soon again on the trail. The incident was passed lightly, with a few jibes at Eldridge, who had quite a reputation for small-time "salvage" of things to eat around the houses at which we stayed. Bill had discovered that in some Albanian garrets small pieces of ham were hung on strings and, when he found such a place, could not resist the urge to cut some of the pieces down and fry them in his mess kit for a midnight snack. I can see him yet, a huddled figure before the dying embers of the hearth, and hear the soft hiss of the ham in the pan as he turned it. It was just that Bill figured we were in tough luck, up against it, and such stuff was fair game. A habit common to soldiers from the beginning, and one quickly acquired and supplied by all recruits.

Less than an hour out from the resting place, snow flakes were in the air and the wind was rising sharply. As we struggled on, the storm thickened and we were forced to turn our heads from the swiftly driving flakes. The storm shut us in on all sides, visibility was reduced to ten feet or less and we had to stay close together to keep from wandering off the trail and becoming lost. The snow became slippery underfoot and in the blinding smother we fell many times. Thrasher had a very narrow escape from serious injury in one fall when he slid for several feet and came with an inch of smashing his head against a projecting rock. The minutes dragged on, and there was no let up in the blizzard. The cold was cutting us to the bone; the altitude cut our breath until we were gasping. We staggered along, falling, crawling forward on hands and knees over places too slippery for us to keep our feet.

Dim figures suddenly bunched into a knot on the trail in front of me. It was Lt. Jean Rutkowski, down in the snow and not getting up. I'd expected it to be Lt. Kopsco, who was especially sensitive to altitude (Mt. Tomorrit has an altitude of 8,136 feet, one of the highest peaks in Albania).

"The hell we will," Baggs was shouting as I came up. "We're all going through! Come on, you'll make it once you're up. You must keep moving, Jean. We all must keep moving!"

"No," Rutkowski gasped, "I can't take another step! Go on! Go on! Just let me stay here. I don't want to go on!"

"Get up!" roared Baggs above the howl of the storm, "You're going to make it! Are you going to sit here and say you're the only one who can't make it? Come on, up you go now!"

He was leaning over her, trying to lift her up and at the same time keep his feet on the slippery snow. Paul Allen bent quickly from the opposite side and between them they managed to bring the Detroit girl to her feet, still protesting that she wanted to be left. Baggs paid no heed, shouting for some raki or alcohol, but nobody had any.

We beat our way onward, holding to the trail only by the swiftly drifting tracks of the rest of the party who had gone on, oblivious to the incident. It seemed as through we could never catch them, that the tracks would soon be completely snowed in and we would be without a guide mark of any kind. But at last we stumbled into them, halted by a crag of dark rock that towered upward and out of sight in the murk of swirling snow.

"Thank God you waited for us," I heard Lt. Jensen say to Thrasher. The pilot looked at her queerly.

"Yeah," he said, "we're waiting."

Then we got the bad news. Our Albanian guide squatted on his heels in the snow. Steffa, swinging his arms to beat warmth into his body, paced up and down, followed by a file of enlisted men cussing and slowly freezing to death in their light clothing.

"We're lost," C.B. said bluntly. He waved a hand at our guide. "He claims we've got to wait the storm out so he can get his bearings."

"Wait hell!" Baggs shouted, "We've got to get Rutkowski out of here! She's done in. Are we going to sit here on our behinds when this storm's liable to last three, four days? We have got to move and keep moving. I don't give a damn where we are or where we come out, we've got to keep going! Let me talk to that damn fool!"

The two pilots went after Steffa and Steffa went after the Albanian. Language flowed from Steffa like the plunging torrent of one of his native streams. The guide's body swayed from side to side in a grim refusal to budge. Steffa launched a new flight of oratory, to no avail. We crowded around, ready to back him with mayhem, only hoping it would come soon. Steffa stood back, panting, and wiped his nose on his sleeve. Then his jaw set in a rock-like line, his bushy brows drew together in a deep scowl. Suddenly he thrust his face down to within inches of the guide's nose and began speaking in a lowered tone. We couldn't understand any of it but, somehow it became perfectly clear to us that friend Steffa was talking sudden death.

The guide got all the words and they went deep enough this time to bring him to his feet. I'll always believe that Steffa told him that if he didn't get up and give us some action right then the patriots would kill him. And in Albania when the patriots say they are going to kill a man, they kill him. The sands run out very quick.

We were soon under way again, but with leaden hearts, because, though we were moving, we knew our steps were taking us no place. I think that at the time most of us expected death was within the hour for the whole party. But we kept going, slipping, falling, crawling fighting the whip of the wind and snow, our minds numbing along with our bodies, until the reality of things began to face and we fought on instinctively, out on our feet, punch drunk, but determined to keep on trying until the lights went out.

That moment never came. What did happen was that the storm blew itself out and we found ourselves in a world of dazzling white, broken only by dark up thrusts of rock. Off a little way, the peak of the mountain, eternal, forbidding, and deadly cold, stabbed at the gray sky. Our guide soon found a narrow pass that skirted the peak. A short time later we knew we were on the down trail, and the gods had smiled. Our spirits revived more swiftly than our frost-stiffened hands and feet. Long before we had passed out of the snow-belt, we could see houses in the valley below us. Coming down that trail, Adams, who was walking beside me, spoke for all of us.

"Orville," he said, with a rueful shake of his head, "I don't ever want to look at any more mountains as long as I live, except maybe on a picture post card."

By the time we reached the village we had been on the trail only about six hours, but time is no measure of living when the going is like that. We were met and warmly received by the president of the council and several residents of the town. They could not believe that we had come over the mountain in the storm and told us that people had lost their lives on the same trail in mid-summer. They wanted to hold a celebration for us, but Thrasher voided it by saying we did not want to impose on them. While we were going through these formalities a large white dog appeared, walking in solemn dignity

90

around the edges of the crowd. Finally one of our gang noticed him backing away, his head jerking up and mouth popping open. He was going through all the motions of barking, but not a sound came from his throat. So, this village will always be remembered by us as "the place of the voiceless dog." The beast, like all Albanian dogs, was vicious and later made an attack on Allen but Paul managed to bluff his way out.

Arriving in groups at our billets we faced the inevitable cornbread, goat's milk, goat soup menu, but downed it without comment. It was too good to be alive and warm again. The only taint to this feeling was the discovery that the cold hadn't killed off our lice and fleas. At our place we took off our clothes and sat around the fire place, picking the fat gray backs out of our underwear and flipping them into the live coals where the quick sizzle and pop they made gave us deep satisfaction. We were all infested with them, even though we made a practice of sleeping in our clothes and pulling our socks up over the outside of our pant legs, in hopes we could keep some of the pests out.

November 24, 1943, Wednesday – morning – Terlioria

We remained over night here and C.B. left word with us that he would send someone around to give us the plans next day. Nurse Rutkowski and others of the party who were near the rope's end on the narrowing trip over the mountain seemed to be making rapid recovery, but we were all in need of rest, warmth, and food. The people at this place were very kind to us. We had a better than usual night's sleep and enjoyed a morning free of our daily stint on the trail. Thrasher himself, coming to our billet at three in the afternoon, found us in good spirit and ready for orders to carry on. We could see that C.B. was excited about something and without wasting time for greeting or even a "How'd you pass?" which had become our standard "Good morning," he fished a folded sheet of paper out of his flying jacket.

"Some really great news fellas," he announced, "we've got a note from the British agent!"

We crowded around him while he read the note aloud, hardly breathing for fear we'd miss a word.

"Sorry to hear of your misfortune," it read, "... the hospital at Catania has been informed of your whereabouts - wheels are in progress for your swift evacuation to civilization."

The note said that the names of our party, listed by Thrasher, had been given to Catania. It also gave us definite instructions for the route we were to take to make contact with the British. When C.B. had finished we let out a wild cheer that brought our Albanian host rushing, wide-eyed, into the room to see if the "crazy" Americans had really gone crazy. He found us in a round of hand shaking and back slapping, with everybody shouting and jumping around. This left him still in some doubt as to our sanity, but it was obvious that no one was being killed. After assuring himself that it was all in good fun and that we were quite normal for Americans, he rose magnificently to the occasion by breaking out a bottle of raki.

One of the biggest loads we had carried was now lifted from our minds and hearts. The best news of all was that word would be going out to the folks back home that we were alive and not in the hands of the Nazis. I thought of Mom, there in our little house on the hill, where the whistle of the night southbound calls loudly from the deep cut of the Muskegon and interrupts the ticking of the clock in the kitchen. Whatever news she had, she was going to get some that was good. Walt was somewhere in Egypt; Bernard was with the tanks in Italy; Clare, the youngest of us, was in a tank battalion out in the Mojave. Four quarters of the earth from which the news might come. But Mom isn't sitting home, waiting for it. She was doing her stint in a war plant, as good a soldier as any of her boys will ever be.

Our outlook, black as the pit and utterly hopeless as we fought the blizzard only twenty four hours ago; was now as bright and promising as a summer sunrise. We were ready for anything now, and nothing could stop us. Ebers and I spent the evening building plans for our escape, and beautiful pictures of what we would do and how we'd work things out when we got back to Sicily. We might even get to go back to the States. At this point, Cranson broke in to promise that he'd get us both drunk WHEN we got back to the States.

Paul Allen prowled around the room, a dreamy grin on his face. "Wheels are in progress," he kept repeating, "swift evacuation - wheels are in progress. That's us! We've been thrown a winner! Wheels are in progress. By God, maybe we get to ride out in trucks, huh?"

10 – Wheels In Motion For Rescue

November 25, 1943, Thursday, morning - Terlioria

We awoke the next morning to find our mountain home shut in by grey fog and a chill drizzle of rain. But we ate our breakfast with gusto and plunged out into the weather with a song, splashing along the muddy trail at a dog-trot as we headed for the meeting place.

"Looks like you might get that Mauser back, Bob," MacKinnon chirped.

"And maybe they haven't had time to kick the hell out of our mandolins, hey Orville?" J.P. suggested cheerily.

"Wheels are in progress---swift evacuation," Allen gloated, in time with his steps.

We found the rest of the gang in the same jubilant spirits. The rain and cold were nothing today. Everybody was anxious to get going and we were soon strung out along the trail, keeping in larger groups than usual, chattering joyously, and now and then raising a song, as we worked down the slope of the mountain. We were heading for Lovdar, the village named in the British note. Steffa trudged along with us, Mohamet like a shadow at his side.

"You must all shave the beards," Steffa announced suddenly.

"What with?" somebody yelped.

"I have the razor," Steffa said, nodding, "po, po, po! You look now like what you call---hell? The people ask of me 'what are these American'-----," he used an Albanian word I suppose meant tramps or bums. "I have to talk, talk, and talk all the time. They laugh when I try to say these are the fine, strong, young soldiers the Americans will send to drive the Germans from Albania."

Judas! We thought back over the places where we had stayed. We felt the lice playing tag around our ribs. If we looked like bums to them, with our scraggly beards and rumpled, weather stained clothing, what did they think they looked like to us? The whole damned country was a hundred years behind the times in sanitation, transportation, commerce and pretty near everything else. But we were too happy to fight with anybody that morning. We looked at each other.

"A shave wouldn't hurt YOU any!"

"Who says, you lousy buzzard!"

"If I had a razor I wouldn't know whether to shave you or cut your throat. No guy should go on living if he's going to look like that."

"And with that fuzz of yours in front of me I'd beg to be put out of my misery!"

"So what, so what?" somebody yelled, and then began,

"Oh what do you know in the infantry?"

And a dozen or more lusty but far from tuneful voices took up the chant. We tramped along in the rain, shouting our lungs out and feeling tops.

"Sure and be jabbers," yelled Cruise exultantly, "the gods be with us this day!"

The march was longer than usual but when we reached our destination we were still feeling good. We had talked over the matter of shaving and had come to the conclusion that we would save our moustaches, and Paul Allen decided he would continue his sideburns to qualify him as a Kentucky colonel. Hayes, with his reddish stubble, knitted wool hat, and bushy brows, looked as though he could have come straight from the crew of Henry Morgan.

"Never will I turn my back on you, my boy," declared Cruise, as the big Iowan stood with feet spread and his thumbs hooked into his belt, a devilish twinkle lighting his eyes.

In this town was a small company of women patriot soldiers and as we were split into groups for the billets, one of these female warriors was told off as guide. Owen, Paul Allen, Jim Cruise, and I set off with a robust damsel, who, like all the others, had a well-worn but efficiently cared for rifle slung by its strap from her shoulder. Pretty soon Owen gave us as a "watch this" look and stepped forward to walk beside our guide.

"You speak English?" he began, turning a smile on her. The girl simply kept walking down the trail.

"No." croaked Cruise from our rear rank, "She no spikk'a da English."

"How'd you like to take it from here, Paul," Bob suggested.

"I will if her old man is having pork chops for supper." Paul shot back.

"The situation appears to call for a shortening of the line, as we say in the Catskills," Owen observed, philosophically. He fished around in his pocket and brought out tobacco and papers, rolled a cigarette, and then offered it to our Amazon.

"Cigarette, mam'selle?"

She understood that all right. For a moment her dark eyes met Bob's and there was the touch of a smile about her lips. She took the cigarette, popped it into her mouth and stepped off the trail to light it, standing with her back against the trunk of a large tree. Through the wisps of smoke she stared at us and we stared back.

"Well," I said, "go ahead and kiss her, she's waiting for you."

"I don't know if she is," Owen said doubtfully, "but if one of you guys will get hold of that gun, I'll try it out."

"You have the bloodiest ideas," Cruise remarked.

"Damn you Bob," Allen complained, "I'm getting hungry! You have no more chance of making it with that gal than I have of setting my teeth in hog meat."

The dark eyes from behind the cigarette never wavered; the girl's expression showed not a flicker of change, but it was far from blank. With cool interest and utterly unafraid, she was simply giving four American soldiers the once over. She just had us faded, that was all. Our eyes followed the arc of the cigarette as she flipped it away.

"Well, that's one you guys don't get butts on," Owen said. He shrugged. "Didn't even save me a drag," he added. "Oh, well."

"Yeah, muttered Allen, misunderstanding him, "that's what I say, "a couple of hells."

We marched down the trail in deep silence for awhile. Then Jim Cruise began to laugh.

"O, Romeo," he cackled, "wherefore art thou Romeo? You ought to be Mahomet!"

Reaching the house where we were to stay, our guide raised her clenched fist to her forehead.

"Vedeke Faschisme!" she said.

We manfully punched our brows.

"Liri Populi!" we chorused.

"And so is your old man," breathed Owen, as we watched the lady solider trudge back down the trail.

November 26, 1943, Friday, morning – Arriving in Lovdar

We were off to an early start next morning. It was rotten weather again, mist so heavy it beaded our flight jackets and then soaked them through. The light stir of air was sharp, sending waves of goose pimples over us when we stopped for rests. But the wet and cold failed to cool our spirits and we made good progress for about three hours. By this time we were overdue at the next village and Steffa and Handlebars held a conference. The party, moving in groups along the trail, rallied around the two as they came up. We rested and rolled some smokes while the Albanians got their bearings and then set off again.

In another hour or so we neared a village and the guides halted us. Steffa had the idea, or at least we gave him credit for it; that we should form ranks and march in with as much a show of military pomp as we could muster. Likely Steffa had sent word ahead that the American expeditionary forces to Albania was about to arrive. Maybe it was only that Steffa had a woman there. I never found out. Our officers, pilots and nurses were to march in front.

"Don't forget to smile," Bill Eldridge kidded Schwant and Tacina as they went by us to the head of the column.

"Maybe there'll be a band out for us," we called after them. At the last minute, in order to make a longer procession I suppose, it was decided that we would march in single file. So we reached the head of the village street and then started down it, stepping out as smartly as we could. It was probably pretty sloppy drill, but it made no difference whatever because there was no cheering section out. In fact not a soul was out; there wasn't even a dog to yap at us. When Steffa finally got somebody rounded up, it appeared that this was an Albanian holiday and most of the people had gone to another town for a celebration.

In due course; however, billets were assigned, and Thrasher, Baggs and Steffa decided to go on to the next place, leaving Mohamet and Johnnie with us, and taking Handlebars with them as guide. Lt. Dawson began to laugh as soon as they were out of earshot.

"That Steffa!" she chuckled. "Anybody want to bet we're not supposed to be in this village at all? And I'll swear that same sap that leaps in the veins of Mortimer Snerd nourishes that guide of ours!" She laughed some more. "The blind leading the blind," she went on, "neither of them knew what town this was. They both thought it was the place where the celebration was going on."

"Right," agreed Owen, "and I'll kill that Handlebars first chance I get."

"Oh, well," Dawson said soothingly, "it doesn't matter as long as we meet the British agent tomorrow."

"It'll be good to see a Limey (slang for British sailors) again," Hornsby said.

"I have a hunch," Cruise announced gloomily, "that we'll miss him...something will happen. And even if we do connect, they'll take six weeks to get us out of here."

"More like three months," growled Adams, digging in his ribs for an over-energetic louse.

"Hell," snorted Allen, who never lost an opportunity to disagree with Adams, "you two buzzards don't know a damn thing more about it than we do. That's nothing but bull---frog music," he finished, with a quick gulp and a roll of his eyes towards the nurses. A snicker went through the group of enlisted men, but Adams wasn't satisfied.

"He said it was a hunch," didn't he?" prodding Paul. "Why don't you wait and see?"

"Same to you!" yelled Allen, his voice cracking on the last word as he clamped off the profane expletive he was about to couple to the advice. "You're always popping off with that big mouth of yours. Listen! How far we from salt water? That's where we have to go, isn't it? We are not fifty miles. That's three days. We meet this Limey tomorrow, and we're back in Italy in three days!"

"Distances are deceptive," Adams said coolly. "You perhaps recall that Hitler's been twenty miles out of England for four years."

Allen lost interest in the argument.

"Well," he said, "the British kept him out. If they can do that good a job, I reckon it won't be so tough for them to get us out of here."

"Oh, sure," Adams scoffed, "just a little walk. They'll probably send a brass band along with us."

"Time goes on," observed nurse Dawson, "look how many birthdays we've had since we've been in Albania – Schwant's, Markie's, Tacina's and Hornsby's and how many others?"

"Hope we aren't here for mine," MacKinnon laughed.

"Mine either," I added.

Mac's birthday comes in April and mine in July. Soon the nurses began moving off to their billets and we broke up too. But the argument went on. How long would it take the British to get us out? What odds were offered on the British not being in the next town at all? In the group I was with our voices droned on for hours in the ark of the loft where we lay under the scanty blankets furnished by our host.

November 27, 1943, Saturday – morning Lovdar

At the square next morning we heard the hum of engines in the sky and ducked for cover while a flight of Jerry fighters zoomed low over the town.

"Bad luck," Cruise sighed, shaking his head slowly from side to side.

"Shut up!" Hornsby's voice was a threatening drawl.

"All right, all right," Jim muttered.

We watched the planes dwindle swiftly down to specks against the gray sky and then wink from sight over a mountain.

Our trip was made without further incident and we arrived about noon. Approaching the town we saw some men on the road ahead of us and soon recognized Thrasher in his scuffed and stained leather flying jacket and O.D. trousers; Baggs was there in a white Albanian goona, similar to our Mackinaw coat, which he had picked up at one of our stops. Then there was Steffa and a fourth man, in uniform and wearing a red cap. He proved to be the British officer, Capt. Smith. At recognition of the Englishman, Allen and Cruise literally jumped for joy. It was a jolly meeting for us all, but we were tired, wet, cold and hungry, facts that did not escape Smith.

"Well, well," he said, in his clipped British accent, "come along. We'll all get out of the weather."

Good to hear somebody speaking English as something besides a foreign tongue. We were led to the town hall where Capt. Smith took a place at the door and shook hands with each of us as we entered, giving each a cheery word and a smile. It was strictly British but---the British know how to do such things. He gave Lt. Rutkowski a big apple and the other girls handed her some neat digs about using influence. Anyway, Capt. Smith didn't read us the history of the British Isles before bringing up the subject of getting us out of Albania.

"We shall make plans to take you out by sea," he said. "There will be little difficulty from the Nazis, but the trip will be rather long and preparations for it must be made. It will be best for you to remain here three days before coming on to our command post. There you must spend a few days resting and being outfitted, so far as we are able, for the trip.

Capt. Smith took off almost at once for the British headquarters, but before leaving gave Thrasher $400 in gold to pay for our three-day lodging. After he left we made our billet arrangements as soon as possible. We enlisted men were sent to a village about and hour's walk away. From this point Johnnie turned back and we saw no more of him.

I think that most of us spent the most miserable seventy two hours of our lives in that hamlet. The food was poor and there was very little of it. We all had lice and the natives knew we had them, so they wouldn't let us use any but the oldest and poorest blankets they had and there were few that were old and ragged enough to give to us. We kept our fires going as best we could with our skimpy allowance of a green, vine-like wood that smoked and threw very little heat, and I don't think we missed an opportunity to steal additional food and fuel. If we did it was pure oversight and not our intention. We reasoned that $400 in gold should have bought us fair accommodations. The natives, it seemed to us, were out to make a handsome profit on us and we were equally determined that it would be considerably less than they planned it to be. We were surely glad when our stay at that place was over and the party assembled back at the town hall.

December 1, 1943, Wednesday – 10:00a.m.

Heading to Krushove

The weather was far from pleasant, but we had long since given up the idea that we could make a start of any kind in good weather. Nearly always it was raining. This time it was snowing and our shoes were beginning to give out. Some of the men had worn the feet completely out of their socks and had thrown the remnants away. Pulling out on the morning of that third day we had six mules, requisitioned by Capt. Smith to carry our baggage. We got off about ten o'clock and within a short time we were strung out in a long irregular file moving steadily upward on a mountain trail that was ankle deep or more with snow. Several of the boys were lagging, due to further attacks of dysentery, and after a couple of hours it became necessary to put two of them, Owen and Allen, on the mules. The girls were taking the trip with a courage and spirit that was a surprise and at the same time an inspiration to all of us. Their shoes, in many cases, were so far gone as ours, but they stuck to the grind and kept going. Another dragging hour went by and we were forced to halt again because two of the party, Nurse Tacina and Sgt. Bill Eldridge had frozen feet and were unable to continue on foot. Places were made for them on the mules; their feet were wrapped in blankets and coats, and each given a shot of codeine to ease the pain.

Hardly were we under way again when the mule carrying Allen bucked and threw Paul into the snow. The Kentuckian floundered to his feet, took two stumbling steps towards the beast and then fell again. Miserable as we were, we couldn't help laughing. Paul got up, roaring with rage and ready to butcher that mule with his bare hands. But during his ride his feet had been frosted until they were like two heavy bricks attached to the ends of his legs. We let him wallow and cuss until his mad had cooled a little and then loaded him back on the mule. Lt. Kanable was still struggling to keep back her laughter as she gave him a codeine pill. Paul growled that he as perfectly able to mount and ride any damned mule in Albania.

After things quieted down, we pushed along until another of the girls, Lt. Kopsco, who had been on foot all the way, had to give up and was put on a mule. Just how far down the scale of conditions we had slipped was showing clearly on this trip. It wasn't as long as and certainly no more rugged than others we had made; but the long days of being on the march, the inadequate food, exposure to all kinds of weather in our thin clothing, and insufficient rest, had worn us down to where a jaunt like this was the KO for a good many. Lt. Kopsco collapsed and had to be carried inside when we finally dragged into the British headquarters town that afternoon. Owen and Allen were two pretty sick boys and it could be said that nearly all of us were hospital cases, only there wasn't any hospital. The British captain who met us expressed surprise that we had attempted to come through in such weather. He didn't know, and I guess no one except ourselves ever knew or understood how desperately we wanted to get out of Albania. The captain, taking note of our plight, cut his reception short, divided us into two groups and assigned us to rooms.

We huddled about the fire, letting its warmth soak into our chilled bodies and steam the dampness out of our clothes. We squatted around that blaze like a bunch of cave men. Except for cussing now and then, the words stuttered out through our chattering teeth, nobody had anything worth the effort to say. In about twenty minutes a couple of Limey soldiers brought us in some tea and the Albanian women of the household prepared us some kind of hot drink, well spiked with raki. The British passed us some of their cigarettes and these, along with the warmth outside and in, gave us a big lift. Some minutes after they had left, one of the two men who had visited us returned.

"Here you are, Yanks," he said cheerily, "these will help warm your feet now."

For each of us he had a pair of wool socks.

"Getting back some of our lend-lease, by God," growled one of our gang as he held up his pair of socks. They were all one size, about 11 ½ and I guess that's the size they gave the girls too. Where they came from, Britain, America, Albania, and Germany --- we didn't know and cared less. The feel of those dry wool socks, pulled on over our soaked, icy feet, was luxury beyond expression. We let our tattered shoes steam in a row before the fire while we sat on the floor behind them with our feet stretched out towards the warmth. To wiggle your toes around in the warm rough wool was heaven. We began to relax, drifting into a half dreamy state where, for the moment, we were unfretted by worry for the future or bitterness for the past.

Pretty soon we learned we were to move on to another house while the nurses and the two sick sergeants, Owen and Allen, remained at this place. At the new billet, thirteen of us enlisted men were given a small room while our two officers, Thrasher and Baggs, and Steffa shared another room in the same house. With us we had the meat of a goat, purchased at the last village, and we went at what was left of the carcass like savages, slashing chunks of meat off the bones, spitting it on hastily cut sticks and hardly letting it more than warm through at the fire before we wolfed it down. After the meal we used the uneatable scraps to grease our shoes.

Ready to turn in for the night we found we had about four blankets. Bedclothes for 13 men! When Thrasher and the British captain came in we showed them what we had and voiced our gripe.

"Come along, old chap," said the Englishman to C.B., "We'll fix that."

In about half an hour Thrasher was back, loaded down with blankets. He dumped them on the floor and turned to us, grinning.

"Worth the trip," he said, "just to hear that British Captain tell off the president of the council. Wish I could give it to you just the way it went, word for word. First the guy said he had no blankets and Cap said he jolly well had. Finally this Tommy got real tough about it. Damned if he didn't threaten to have the guy shot at 6 a.m. tomorrow morning if he didn't come through with blankets in the next five minutes. I was standing there trying to look murder, like Cap told me to. I damn near blew a gasket. But it went over. We got them, so get your beauty rests made up and don't let me hear more from you until noon tomorrow. We're going to stay here a few days and try to get some shoes cobbled.

That was news all to the good. We were more than due for some time off. We talked it over and along with it the news given us by the British that Berlin had been heavily bombed night before last. Then we settled down and made a pretty fair night of it.

December 2, 1943, Thursday Krushove

In the morning came a supply of food from the British, powdered eggs, apples and nuts, and a few other items. We unanimously elected Bill Eldridge and Lebo to be our chefs and they accepted, announcing that their policy would be first come, first served --- after the cooks.

We spent the next two days in lazy fashion. We talked over methods of escape in great detail; we laid our lavish and extensive programs for ourselves, once we were returned to allied territory. We played a lot of poker, with the gummy deck of cards one of the boys had in his musette. Then there were the shaving parties, in which each man tried to out-do the others with his comedy barber act, and our faces again took on the semblance of civilization. We even got around to doing some washing and bathing in the stream that flowed close by the house. The weather cleared and was very fine, a change we accepted as a matter of course since we were not on the trail, trying to get somewhere. Our shoes went off to the repair shop in relays, leaving us a few pairs to get around in, those remaining becoming common property for all.

The second day brought Allen and Owen back to our party. They had improved considerably and the report was that up at the other place they were finding too much raki. Paul pulled off his shoes as soon as he came in and then spread his arms to the warmth of the embers on our hearth.

"Well, fellas, sure is swell to be back," he said, "Bob and I really had a close squeak. I didn't know whether ------."

"You're a drunkard!" Lebo hissed in dramatic accents, his hand resting lightly on a hip thrown out at a rakish angle and his nose pointed at the upper northeast corner of our cubicle. Allen grinned sheepishly in the laugh that greeted Lebo's effort.

"It's a damn lie!" he roared good–naturedly. "We never had a drop did we, Bob? Not a drop --- except as medicine, doctor's orders, every drop we had, isn't that right, Bob?"

"Yeah," drawled Owen, "doctors Owen and Allen, specialists in drying up the cornbread----."

"You're damn right," Allen broke in, "the secret is to paralyze the guts, give them a good pickling and you feel like doing the hog wild reel in fast time."

"You not only feel like it," Owen added, "You do it. So ---- here we are!"

"Yeah," Paul went on, "they canned us just when we had everything under control. But I am not too sure about the future without my medicine. Don't any of you touch those shoes! And you better post a man on the door to get it open because ----."

"We have a rule," Shumway interposed, "that a guy owns the first vacant pair of shoes he can get to. Those brogans of yours will be handy. They're so big that all we'll have to do is jump towards them and take off as soon as we light.

With Allen and Owen added to our number, the room, which had been crowded before, became impossible. So, after a night that was downright miserable, we were split into two groups. With some Albanian ferrying shoes for us, we managed to move to different quarters. On this day, also, quite a number of new cases of dysentery developed to a point that wasn't funny. The nurses, bless them, had made a habit of checking on us every day, either at quarters or when we assembled at village squares to begin the trek. When Lt's. Watson, Kanable, and Nelson came to see our sick men that afternoon they found us all pretty low. Our supply of drugs, especially the sulfas, was practically gone now, so the nurses put the worst cases on a beef broth diet and told us to keep them wrapped in blankets.

The nights now were clear and beautiful and the fine weather made it possible for British planes to come over and drop supplies. Those of us who were well enough went out to watch this operation when we heard the mutter of engines growing out of the distance. The first ship missed the mark and when the load was dumped several of the chutes failed to open. So we lost about two thirds of the stuff. But the second ship came in right on the beam and we got practically everything dropped.

December 4, 1943, Saturday - Krushove

The next day word came via radio from Cairo that we were to move on through to the coast as soon as possible and would be picked up by boat. The nurses again visited our sick men and found them showing some improvement. The last batch of shoes was promised for the following day. Everything seemed to be shaping up so that our departure need not be longer delayed. We began to feel that our troubles and disappointments were over and that we'd soon be back with the outfit again. In another twenty four hours our casualties had gained a lot and it was decided to make the start in the morning. That night British cargo plans again thundered over head, huge, black, swift-moving shadows against the moonlit sky. They dropped more supplies and, with them, half-dozen British paratroopers came floating down. Some of these men had been out here before and their first question on meeting the British commander was,

"How're things going, sir?"

"Lively," we heard the captain respond in his soft, clipped accents. "Quite a bit has been all right. And since you've been away," he went on, "we've had ten beautiful American women visiting us."

"Did you say women, sir? American women, sir?" questioned the troopers in amazement.

"Oh yes! Quite so! The captain chuckled. "Too bad," he added, "they'll all be gone tomorrow."

11 – Led By British Lieutenant Gavin Duffy

December 5, 1943, Sunday– morning - Krushove

Our stay in this village brought the re-appearance of our old friend Hassan, who came in with Acorns and a small band of patriot soldiers a day or two after our own arrival. It was good news to us to know that Hassan was going with us on the march to the sea.

"That guy is strictly able," Shumway declared. "He knows what he's doing all the time and no fooling. You can put the blue chips on him any day."

We had rumors of a Captain Lloyd Smith of the American Intelligence office, whom we were to meet somewhere along the way and who would take over command of the party for the final stages of the trip. Thrasher and Baggs immediately concluded that Smith was an officer they knew and were not much impressed with his qualifications for the job, but the matter was then too far in the future to be of any great concern. Our shoes had come back from the cobbler. Mine had a couple of well-worn pieces of automobile tire tacked on for soles and other pairs I saw had fared no better. At the time, it seemed evidence of the extent to which the Germans and Italians had stripped the country. It was not until later that I learned that this was the customary use for old tires in Albania. We sure wished we could step up and draw a good pair of GU shoes for the trip, but it was a case of use what you had and be glad you were not going barefoot. Some of the nurses were in British hobnail field shoes with heavy metal toes and heel plates and others came to this type of footwear as the shoes they had went to pieces on the journey.

The British took charge of all plans for the trip and our only orders were to assemble in front of the quarters occupied by the nurses on the morning of the sixth day. When our squad arrived at the house we saw a couple of mules standing in front of the place, piled high with baggage and equipment which included a portable radio set and several map cases. There were two Albanian patriots, one by the name of Pandee, and then there was the big English sergeant, J.W. Bell, whom we quickly nicknamed Blondie.

In conversation with him as we came up, was an equally husky British lieutenant. This was ruddy, black-browed Gavin (Gary) Duffy, who was to be the leader of our party. Duffy, a six-foot Yorkshire man, was wearing an overseas cap set at a jaunty angle wall back on his thick thatch of dark hair that overflowed into deep sideburns. His scarf was made of a pink parachute panel, a ruffle of color at the opening of his dark, regulation blouse. For the rest there was a leather cartridge belt, the loops all filled, a pair of gray, baggy, British battle-dress trousers, and sturdy, metal cleat, British GI shoes. As he stood talking to Blondie, he held a British Tommy gun across his shoulder, his hand on the barrel, near the muzzle. Thrasher and Baggs appeared, each with an Italian Tommy gun, smaller than our .30 caliber but with a metal stock that made it heavier to carry. The Albanians were armed as usual, except for the mule drivers. At the last minute, three or four additional mules and their drivers came up and what baggage we had left was stowed on them, leaving the saddles open for riders.

December 8, 1943, Wednesday– 10:00 a.m.

Heading to Gjergievice

We said our farewells to the British Intelligence officers and then got under way, Pandee, who spoke English, acting as guide and marching with Lt. Duffy at the head of the column. We fell in, mules and "foot-troops" behind them, and were soon clear of the village. Our spirits were high and we swung along the trail in brisk fashion that morning. A few more days, we believed, would bring us to the sea and then evacuation to the Allied lines. As was most often the case, the group on foot worked rapidly to the head of the column, leaving the mule train strung out behind us. Steffa and Mohamet were out in front with Pandee, the guide, while Hassan and Acorns were at the rear, with the mules. Gary, as we soon came to call Lt. Duffy, drifted up and down the line, seeing that things were in order and moving. It was on one of these trips that some of us got into conversation with him.

"I'm glad enough to be going along with you chaps," he said, "but it means I'll miss out on those executions."

"What executions?" somebody asked.

"Oh, the bally buzzards who've been stealing our supply parachutes. Caught them red-handed, we did."

Gary's thirst for blood shocked us a little, I think. It was another of those times when suddenly the fact of war was driven home to us. It just didn't seem real that several Albanians were to pay with their lives for stealing a few parcels of supplies that had dropped wide of the mark. But that was Gary's story and he stuck to it, although he did say that the men had been turned over to the patriots and the shooting would be done by them.

About an hour out, Lt. Thrasher sighted a flock of large birds passing over head and cut loose at them with his Tommy gun. The firing brought Gary on the run and he didn't seem to think it was funny that C.B. had slammed away at them without hitting a thing. We got the idea that shooting for fun was out. A short time later we stopped to let our straggling caravan close up before entering a village that Duffy told us had been burned by both German and Italian invaders. Some miles away, on the slope of a mountain, etched out with huge boulders, we could see the roughly formed letters V.F. (Vdectkee Facishme) and L P. (Liri Populi). In clear weather, symbols would be visible for a great distance. Some person or group had used a lot of time and muscle to put them there.

In the town, where a few people were living in the charred ruins of what had once been their homes, Gary went into one place and came out with a cartwheel of wheat bread which he broke up and carefully divided among us. We drank some water and smoked some of our "duhan," native tobacco, during a rest of about an hour. Then we pushed on.

Hardly were we under way again when Blondie gave his ankle a bad twist and had to be put on a mule. Only a few yards farther along one of the nurses gave out and me, who had been fighting off an attack of dysentery, also had to be put in a saddle. The trail was not as steep as some we had been on and we were moving down grade over it. But it was very narrow and at times there were places where it pitched down for a short distance on an angle so sharp that the riders had to leave their mules. At these places the Albanian drivers would get a two-handed grip on the mules tail and move slowly down the pitch with their feet braced and their weight thrown back, holding the animal from slipping and landing at the bottom in a heap. We'd never seen this system used, and always speculated on the possibility of both mule and driver starting to slide, but no such incident occurred. The mules were perfectly accustomed to the method and took it quiet as a part of their daily routine.

About four o'clock we arrived in another village, and were divided into groups for billets and spent the evening in the usual fashion, huddled around our fires, talking about home and food.

December 9, 1943, Thursday – 0900 - Heading to Panerit

In the morning we gathered again at the town square ready to push on. But Paul Allen was in a wild fit of temper because the people in the house where he stayed had stolen his parachute cord. He appealed to Gary, asking the use of his Tommy gun.

"Won't take ten minutes," Paul pleaded. "I'll make that lousy so-and-so produce or else! I've hauled those shrouds all over this damned country and I am not going to lose them now!"

Gary grinned and shook his head.

"Fall in, sergeant," he said, "we're ready to march."

But Paul was too angry to be swayed so easily from his purpose.

"All right, go ahead," he yelled, "I'll catch you after I've gone back there and stood that buzzard on his head a couple times. I'll cut both ears off him! He's going to give me that cord, by God, or I'll scalp him!"

Gary swung the muzzle of the Tommy gun towards Allen. He wasn't grinning now.

"Fall in!" he shouted, the color deepening in his face. "I'm in command of this party and I want no trouble. Let's hear no more of your bloody lines!"

For a moment Allen stood irresolute, his eyes fixed on the stern British officer. Then Bob Owen spoke.

"Come on, Paul," he said, in a low voice, "play ball."

The Kentucky boy turned slowly and moved to a place in our line, grumbling to himself. Something about the British having Albanians shot when they stole supplies from the Limey's but giving them a medal if they stole from Americans. But Gary had swung off to the head of the column at once and we were on our way. Paul was never one to carry a grudge and his anger soon cooled.

There was tough going that morning as our trail shifted upward again. We climbed steeply along the face of a cliff and when we at last reached the summit we were all ready to flop for a rest. We spent perhaps an hour there, smoking, talking, and gazing out over what seemed to be endless folds of wooded mountains, fading off into a gray horizon. Somewhere off in that murk we could hear the muffled pound of bombs or heavy guns, but could see no smoke or flashes that would tell us what the action might be.

December 9, 1943, Thursday –5:00 p.m. - Arrival at Panerit

Gary prodded us on again. He was hard as nails, in the pink, and took our daily marches easily. He was always urging us on, always seeming to be in a hurry to get to the next town. We were on the trail eight hours that day, including stops. When we finally pulled into the village of Panerit, a cold rain was beginning to fall and it was dark. The council president was on hand to greet us; however, and led the party to a patriot hospital located in the village. Bill Eldridge was coming down with something and after the long trip looked and acted like a pretty sick boy. But we hoped a night of rest would get him back in shape to travel. There was about an hour's conference at the hospital and then we all went to witness a wedding. After that, we went to our billets and were glad to settle down. At least that's what all but two of us did. Lebo and Shumway got assigned to the newly-weds house where a celebration was going on. We heard about it in the morning.

December 10, 1943, Friday – morning - Leaving Panerit

"Very quiet affair," our crew chief reported, "one bullet went through the ceiling, there was a couple chairs busted up, and three, four guys got cuts and bruises while they were bringing in one of those buffalo. They were going to tie the groom on it. Anyhow that's how it looked to me."

"From under the table," chimed in Lebo. "When that gun went off Shumway fell right off his stool and rolled under there."

"Only way he knows that," Shumway added, "he was already there when it happened. These Albanians sure had themselves a time. Only when I get married I don't want any Albanians mixed in it."

"A little of that raki----," began Lebo.

"Goes a hell of a long ways," finished Shumway. "You ought to know!"

"How was the bride?" somebody suggested, "Any glamour?"

"There were a couple dozen women in the place," Lebo explained, "soldiers and such, but we never did get the bride pointed out to us."

"She would have been twins to you anyhow," Shumway commented. "There were just ten women there, and as for glamour, you guys ought to know by now that we got all the glamour in Albania traveling right with us."

"Those gals could sing though," Lebo declared, "they really went to town with a couple those numbers."

So it went. The wedding carried us over several long miles. Our party was split into two groups for most of the journey that day. The largest group, our "foot troops," were slogging ahead while the rest remained back with the mules, among them Sgt. Eldridge, who was too weak to do more than sit in a saddle.

The rain had stopped but the country was shrouded in heavy fog and the trees dripped ice water down our necks. Just before reaching the village at the end of our four-hour trek, we came to a very swift river and halted to let the mules come up for use in the crossing. The first of the nurses to ford on the mules became dizzy when they looked down at the rush of black water and Steffa, seeing them sway and clutch frantically at the saddle points, shouted advice to them from the bank.

"Keep the heads up," he yelled, "look at the mountain! Look at the mountain!"

Thereafter, as soon as a group of nurses started across, Steffa began shouting these instructions. So as soon as Steffa got aboard a mule and started across he received a volley of yells from both banks.

"Keep your head up! Hey, Steffa! Look at the mountain! Look at the mountain!"

The nurses, officers and Steffa proceeded on immediately to the village while the rest of us saw to getting baggage and equipment across the stream. When this was done, we also pulled out, leaving the mules and drivers to follow. Bill Eldridge and one or two others who were sick or weary of the trail, remained to come on with the mules. We got in about three o'clock. By six it was beginning to rain and an hour later, in a heavy downpour, our mule train arrived. Bill was running quite a temperature and, needless to say, the others were not improved by their hour's ride in the rain. We learned that the river we had crossed was rising rapidly and by eight o'clock it was reported impassable.

"Well," observed Hornsby, "it seems like something is always going to happen to us but nothing ever does."

"Hell," exclaimed Owen, "you're not complaining are you?"

"Just a breeze," drawled Cruise. "This is 'The life of Riley.' It's going to be very tough getting back to evacuation. I don't know how I'll stand it after having things so easy and comfortable all these weeks!"

"Aw, forget it," muttered Hornsby, "I'm keeping my fingers crossed, same as everybody."

Nevertheless, being on the wrong side of that river and having to camp out all night waiting for it to go down would have been serious. We were less and less able to stand rugged weather, and Gary had indicated that our best chances for safety on this trip were to keep moving. We spent a good night in this village. We were treated well and among the villagers we found several who could speak English. This always helped. You always get along better with people you can talk to and understand. Hayes, Pandee, Blondie and I were billeted together and we wrapped Blondie's twisted ankle for him, Hayes promising to carry his rifle for him the next day.

December 11, 1943, Saturday – late morning
Leaving Gostomicka

We got off to a late start in the morning and assembled in a village about an hour's journey along the trail. The council president gave us all a drink of raki. Bill Eldridge had to be carried in. He had passed out completely on the short trip and his fever was still dangerously high. The nurses were doing all they could for him but they didn't try to hide the fact that they were worried.

"I keep thinking about that damn stone," said Cruise, as we sat around and smoked.

"What stone and do I hear anybody call butts on this?" Owen asked. Nobody claimed, and Bob flipped away the stained end of his home-made.

"Why you remember," Cruise went on, "back there by the creek, before we went over that mountain? Those natives said the man who had that stone was going to ----."

"Hells' bells!" roared Allen, "don't fall for that tripe! I know them kind of people. Besides he gave them back their stone, didn't he?"

"Yeah, but they said that didn't make any difference," Cruise insisted.

"The hell it doesn't, Paul declared firmly. "How are you going keep a hex on a guy when he gives it back to you? You can't make a hex stick unless ----- what are you guys laughing at?"

"Don't fall for that tripe!" Owen gibed.

Paul stared at him. Then he scowled and shrugged.

"All right, all right," he grumbled, "Only I say there's no hex on Bill. I keep telling you guys it's this lousy cornbread and goat we've been getting. If we could put Bill on a diet of pork chops a couple days he'd befit as a wildcat. Goat---goat," he declaimed, "Nothing but goat! We get all but the hair and horns. I am telling you there's times when it doesn't even stop there. Man isn't built to live on mutton alone, says so in the Bible, anyhow, Americans are not!"

This was Paul's plaint, any time, day or night. But, since his upset, back before we reached British headquarters, he belied his preaching and was healthier than most of us. We went to several houses to have dinner and at our place we each got a spoonful of honey with the meal. It sure tasted good, but we were anxious to know what the decision on Bill would be, so hustled through with the food

---

and got back as soon as we could. In our talk about it the feeling grew that as long as Bill was alive he was staying with the party and we were sticking by him, even though it meant staying right where we were until the Germans came and got us.

We were not put to that test, because it was decided that Bill, sick as he was, could be moved and would go on with us. Leaving the village we split into two groups, the mules and riders taking one route and we of the "foot troops" another. Gary led us at a fast pace, although several of the girls were with us. We pushed along until four in the afternoon when a hard rain slowed us down, but on through ankle-deep mud and water we went. Lt. Baggs and Hassan were acting as rear guard for the column and, shortly after the rain started Baggs came up along the line at a trot, spreading the word that a friend in the last village had told Hassan that the Americans had landed in Albania and were driving inland.

God! How we wanted to believe that news. We all tailed Baggs up to where Gary and C.B. were setting the pace. This bit from Hassan confirmed a rumor of a night or two before, that invasion of the Balkans was imminent. Those guns or bombing raids we'd been hearing from time to time added evidence to the story. We gathered in an excited group around Gary, everybody talking at the same time, trying to make him understand the news. The British officer's eyes smoldered and a red flush crept into his cheeks.

"A lot of damned rot," he declared loudly, "bally nonsense, that's what! Stop acting like a lot of crazy fools!"

Thrasher protested, "But Gary! Everything checks. This is the best news we've had since we hit Albania! Why don't we set up the radio and get Cairo for confirmation?"

Gary Duffy's temper flared then. He really burned the air around there, paying no heed to what anybody said. Among the mildest of his remarks was the repeated advice not to get heated over a "bloody rumor." From it all we gathered that if invasion had been coming, Cairo would never have cleared our start for the coast. And if, by the wildest and most foolish stretch of the imagination, something more than a night commando foray had landed, we were in for it because it would mean German reinforcements pouring into Albania and quick tightening of the Nazi net all about us.

Gary's words simply went in one ear and out the other for us then. We knew our gang was coming to meet us, pounding their way inland, making our trip shorter, and kicking the hell out the Jerries we'd been dodging all these weeks. Nobody could talk or shock us out of it. It was wonderful. It was beautiful. Jim Cruise threw his arms around the nurses nearest to him, who happened to be Markie, and jumped up and down with her in the mud and water.

"Please be true!" he shouted tears and rain flowing down his cheeks, "it must be true! Please God; it's got to be true!"

The he let Markie go and dug vigorously with both hands into his lice–bitten ribs.

12 – Climbing Another Mountain
Mt. Nermerska

December 11, 1943, Saturday –5:00 p.m. - Arrival in Malinj

We carried on through the wet. Some of us were in high spirits, feeling that surely the great day had come and the long anticipated drive through the Balkans for a junction with the Russian front had begun. Others of the party, not so optimistic, plodded along in silence, as if fearing that anything they might say would bring bad luck. A few had swung to Gary's side, although they made no attempt to convince the others.

We arrived at our destination at five o'clock, met the head man of the village, and were taken to a schoolhouse where a fire was blazing on the open hearth. Within a few minutes our mules came into town, carrying Sgt. Eldridge, nurses, and a few enlisted men. A short time later we were all in our billets. Blondie went to work with his radio set to make contact with Cairo, and we spent an anxious evening waiting for further word of the invasion. Of course no such news came.

December 12, 1943, Sunday – 9:00 a.m. - Leaving Malinj

At the schoolhouse the next morning the thought of word from Cairo was uppermost in our minds. Only the officers knew what had come in or gone out over the radio. There was nothing now to show any change had been made in our plans. We watched Thrasher closely for some sign or word. But there was nothing. He seemed rather blue and talked hardly at all. Gary and Blondie were about their usual chore of packing the mules. Taking it all in, none of us had the heart to put our question into words. If the news had been good, C.B. would have spilled it before this. It just wasn't good.

Still raining, not hard, but plenty wet. We hit the trail in glum silence, taking the rap as best we could, but not making too good a go of it at the start. It was too bitter a disappointment to us then, though later we all admitted that Gary had probably been right in saying that an invasion would have made our position much more difficult and dangerous. About an hour out Sgt. Zieber began singing in his melodious baritone and was joined by Lt. Thrasher. The rain slacked and stopped and the solid overcast of the sky began to break up, letting patches of sunlight sift through. With the harmony of our two troubadours and the clearing weather, our morale climbed out of the basement and we began to be Americans again. The trip to the next village was short; we arrived about 10 o'clock, and our luck, given a thorough kicking around that morning, proved surprisingly good just when we were most in need of a lift. The place was one of the best we found in the whole of our wanderings. The people were especially friendly and kind, giving us good food and saw that we had good places for the night. We awoke the next morning with a new outlook on life.

December 13, 1943, Monday – 09:30 a.m. - Leaving Odrican

Assembling at the square; some of us gathered around a tiny blacksmith shop and watched the smith at his work while we waited for our mules to be packed. About the only blacksmith shop most of us knew was the one that stood, "under the spreading chestnut tree." Our streak of luck was holding, for it was clear and a fine day for traveling. We took off about 9:30 and after a hike of forty five minutes stopped in a ravine for cigarettes and a rest. While there, Gary snapped a picture of us. Taking the trail again, Lt. Watson asked, "How far to the next village? Anybody know?"

"Yes ma'm," Jim Baggs announced, "I reckon it's just about four hours as the crow flies with an Allison engine."

Everybody had a laugh over that and we pushed on. Within a short time we came to a very small village and as we were going through, Watson didn't miss having her say.

"That Allison surely improved your crow's flying time," she reminded Baggs. Jim grinned.

"Just can't believe it no how," he drawled.

On the outskirts of this place we stopped to rest again and a number of the boys took to the bushes, I being one of them, who have had a lot of fun with the dysentery when Paul Allen had it. The party pulled out without waiting for the missing sergeants to rejoin them. An hour later, Paul asked for a halt and informed the officers that I was still missing.

I was making it all right, but I didn't feel like doing any running. We were on a gravel road, a main highway between Albania and Greece so I knew I'd just have to keep plugging along it until I caught up with the party. Quite a few natives were on the road and most of them spoke to me, some stopping to talk. They talked Albanian and I talked English, so the conversation didn't amount to much but the Albanians wanted to get a look at me and I was doing the same to them, although by now the sight of an Albanian was nothing new to any of us.

"Shake it up, Orville," Paul yelled, as I came in earshot of where the party had been halted by the collapse of a mule. They were ready to move again and I waived them on.

"Go ahead," I yelled back, "I'm O.K."

They pushed along while I struggled. Then, near the town we were heading for, a blown bridge over the Vjose River, a fairly wide river held them up. This brought me back into the fold again without extra effort. We were told that patriots, defending the town, had blown the bridge, suspended on wires provided a crossing for pedestrians but our mules had to be unpacked and led down to a fording place a few yards below the bridge. When the crossing had been completed, we found that a truck had been sent out to bring us into the city.

We stood in the body of the truck while it rolled slowly along a road on which the scars of war were numerous. The place had been burned by both the Italian and German invader. At the edge of town quite a large group of patriot soldiers were quartered in a ruined barracks that had once housed Italian occupation troops. The patriots lined the roadside, waving and shouting, "Americano!" at us. On the other side of the road there was a cemetery where we saw a number of grave markers that were like those on the graves of Italian fliers at Berat.

December 13, 1943, Monday - Permet

The patriot leader who welcomed us directed the truck to the center of town. We all got down and were taken into a large barroom where our host proceeded to order shots of raki for those who wanted it, wine for those who didn't, and both for those who could take it. Then there was a big basket of grapes, some cheese and some wheat bread. Thrasher bought some tobacco and papers and passed them around. Everything seemed to be plentiful, but we later found that the people were very poor and that food was expensive and not easy to get. We stayed in the bar, enjoying our welcome, for about two hours and then were assigned to billets. At this place there was a telephone line connected with a British station on the other side of the mountain. Our instructions had been to put a call through on our arrival, but we found the line had been broken.

December 14, 1943, Tuesday – morning - Leaving Permet

In the morning Lt. Baggs visited us, presenting each with a napoleon, (about $1.00 in American money) Albanian money. With this fund we went into the market seeking fruit for our breakfast, and fared according to our ability as traders. Anyone who used the American system of asking the price, putting down his money, and walking out with his purchase, didn't get much for breakfast. You always refuse the first price, which is a big joke; you give up in despair on the third; then you get a little bit interested on the fourth and perhaps buy on the fifth or sixth offer. We had risen early and it was only about nine when we assembled at the barroom. Our trail led over the mountain to Shepr, the place we couldn't reach by phone.

In a much smaller village along the way we caught sight of a little old man with a white beard and somebody called,

"Hey, look! Here comes Kris Kringle!"

To our surprise the old man stopped and waved at us.

"Hi, comrades," he yelled, "I am happy to see you! Welcome, welcome! I was in America once."

"Where did you live in America, grandpa?" asked Lt. Markowitz sweetly.

"I lived in Chicago!"

"And why did you leave?" asked Bob Owen, with sarcasm, then, as his New York complex asserted itself, he added, "as if anybody needs an excuse to leave Chicago."

"Crazy!" shouted the old man. "I was crazy! There is only one country in the world where a man should live. That is America!"

We shouted and laughed our approval as we pushed on, leaving him staring after us. Yes, that is the lesson every GI Joe learns very quickly, and I think that is the lesson we bring back with us. There are good people and bad, everywhere. There are great things, things we heard about in school, to see. But there is only one place to live --- that's home! We learned that lesson especially well, even though we are eternally indebted to our Albanian and British friends for the help they gave us. When you are with the American army, wherever you go, you have a little bit of home with you. That's something you don't realize until you get to wandering around homeless, like we were, in a strange land. Home was an obsession with us. We talked about it constantly, home and food. Its nearest border was the American lines, but deep, far back, there was the heart of it all, that fabulous, heavenly land called the United States of America.

The trail led sharply upward and we were soon on one of the toughest climbs we had, so steep that we had to stop and rest at the end of every hard-won hundred yards or so. At one of these stops, Zieber pulled off his tattered shoes. His reddened toes and heels poked through great holes in his socks. He stripped the ragged remnants off and threw them away, putting his shoes back on over his bare feet. We watched in silence. It was what we were all coming to.

The first of our party to come out on top of Mt. Nermerska, (an altitude of 8,186 feet) were Nurses Dawson and Kanable, a fact we all noted because it was these two who usually seemed rather sensitive to altitude and who were often the ones we had to stop and wait for on trails well up in the mountains.

December 14, 1943, Tuesday –3:00 p.m. - Arrive in Shepr

The down trip to Shepr was made without incident, taking about three hours, and on arrival we were greeted by an English speaking Albanian who took us to the quarters of a British major. Here we received a hearty welcome and were taken into his rooms where we had a radio and some magazines. Cigarettes were passed and very soon we had some hot tea. It was very cozy and brought a life to our famished spirits along with rest and warmth for our bodies.

Our officers and the British went into conference on plans for our future operations, but for once we didn't care how long they talked. We liked it there, looking at the magazines with the sound of the radio in the background. All too soon it was announced that ten enlisted men were to move on to a village an hour away and then come back in the morning.

December 15, 1943, Wednesday – 0900 - Leaving Shepr

Before we left we said good-bye again to our old friend Hassan and his pal, Acorns. They were returning to their own bailiwick, where, we understood, their service was needed. We knew that meant dead Germans, and that suited us. But we were sorry to see Hassan go. We never saw him again. I wonder where he is now. He was a guerrilla fighter, and I'd rate him tops among all we saw in Albania. But no matter how good a man is in his business of war, there is the hour and the minute when his number may be up. I hope that time never comes for Hassan in this war. But he lived with danger day and night, accepting the one rule of, "kill or be killed," as a matter of course. I, for one, will never forget him nor relinquish the hope that I may some day repay a part of our debt to him.

We enlisted men set out on the one-hour tramp, flogging our luck in real army fashion as we trudged along. We worked up to the conclusion that we were heading for the gloomiest hole in all creation, a place that would not have enough food in it to keep a couple of brass monkeys from starving to death. Wrong again! We sat down to a really nice dinner, and we were completely bewildered at finding beds that were comparatively comfortable. It was all very much worth the extra hike, and our Lady Luck, after taking such a beating on the way out, was fully restored to favor. We rose early, after a good sleep, and walked back to Shepr to meet our comrades, knowing that however well they had fared, they had nothing on us except the walking.

At nine o'clock the mules were packed and dozing in front of the British mission. Our party was assembled and ready. Ahead of us was a nine-hour journey and we were anxious to be off. The trail, as we settled into the grind, was an upgrade, but the angle was not too steep for good traveling. Midway of the trip, Sgt. Bill Eldridge, who had been on a mule during our movements for several days, but who was making rapid progress towards recovery, got off the beast he was riding and again joined the "foot troops." As the day wore on, the party became split, due to the pace set by Gary for the marchers and the slower gait of the mules and some of our numbers who were not able to keep up with the advance. Thrasher, Baggs and Steffa remained with the second group.

December 15, 1943, Wednesday – 8:00 p.m. - Mashkulon

At dusk, we were in sight of the city we had been working towards all day. A mile out of town we came upon an air field that had once been used by the Italians but was not abandoned. As we crossed the field, a terse command came suddenly from Gary.

"Down!" he ordered. Then, "Move over along that fence and stay there."

He had spotted a motor vehicle moving along the road that led out of the city and was taking no chances that it might be a Jerry patrol car. We lurked in the shadows along the fence until the machine had passed, its light sending a yellow glow through the twilight, and the sound of its motor throbbing into the distance along the roadway.

"What was it?" we questioned. "Was it German?"

"Don't know," Gary replied curtly, his eyes on the road. He seemed to think that was answer enough, and I suppose it was. Any motor vehicle was dangerous to us because motor transport was mostly in Nazi hands, especially the machines that were in good operating condition. The stuff we rode in was worn out, dilapidated, and always seemed about to give a last wheeze before stopping forever.

Gary led us along a side road to a bridge and there we took cover until dark. The main road, on which the car had recently passed, followed the farther bank of the stream. After dark, we crossed to the road and moved into town to the patriot headquarters, located in a schoolhouse of quite modern design. Inside, we sat around and visited while we waited for our officers and the rest of the party to show up. After waiting a half hour Gary took over and made the arrangements for billets. We were about to take off when others arrived, relieving the anxiety we had begun to feel about them.

December 16, 1943, Thursday – 10:00 a.m.
Heading to Zhulat

The next morning when we arrived at the school house we found a large detachment of patriot soldiers gathered there. They were singing and appeared to be in high spirits while they awaited orders for the march. Some of us had gifts and oranges purchased on the market for us by our hosts. Thrasher gave money to several of the nurses and they brought back more figs and some nuts. So we made our breakfast. Meanwhile, the patriot soldiers formed their column and marched off down the road. We didn't know where they were going, but the thought came that these men might soon be fighting Germans, perhaps some of them would be dead tomorrow, but we knew they'd take the toll of the enemy these hardy, mountain fighters always expected.

At ten o'clock we too moved out, heading for a village two hours away from the main road. Gary remained behind, hoping to set up radio contact with Cairo and investigating further a report that a Nazi Gestapo agent was in the city and that he had sent for a company of Jerries to come and make us prisoners. In the little parley we held before leaving, Thrasher approached Gary with a plan we had all been thinking and talking about.

"If you're contacting Cairo," he said, "why can't a deal be made to put a transport plane on that air field back there? It would be the quickest way out for us, and God knows we need some help. We can't keep up this walking forever. It'd take us off your hands too."

Gary shook his head slowly.

"We don't know how much of the stuff we send through is being intercepted," he pointed out. "If we tried a scheme like that it jolly well might mean a hot reception for your chaps when they got here. And if it didn't, the Huns would make these people here pay bloody well for letting you get out."

Another of our bright dreams wiped out. Riding back in a C53, the way we came in, was no go. We argued about it and groused plenty, but we had to resign ourselves to more of the same old walking around Albania.

December 16, 1943, Thursday – 1:00 p.m. - Arrival in Zhulat

On the outskirts of the city we came upon a small dam and filled our canteens from the pool. Then we settled into our pace and made the trip without incident. We were all on foot, as the mules had been left to be brought on by Gary and Blondie. At our destination we found the village had been burned several times by the Italians during

Mussolini's war in Albania, and the people were living in the patched up remnants of the homes left standing after the ebb and flow of battles had passed. Food was not plentiful, but C.B. was able to buy a young calf and two ducks shortly after our arrival at one o'clock.

Johnny Wolf dispatched the calf and butchered out the meat for us. Lt. Baggs became lord high executioner for the ducks, and we all gave a hand where it was needed. The veal was portioned among the men and the ducks were given to the nurses. In spite of our cramped and rather broken down quarters, we had some good food and made a fair night of it. The weather had held good for the past few days and that helped.

December 17, 1943, Friday - Zhulat

Gary and our mule train did not come in during the night and in the morning there was still no sign of the British or word from them.

"The Gestapo's got them," Cruise predicted. "Something's happened to them or they'd be here."

"Nuts," scoffed Shumway, "they've got rid of us and are probably having themselves a time back in that town."

But when noon passed with still no appearance, we were all pretty well convinced that we'd seen the last of Lt. Gary Duffy and that the Jerries had him. It made many of our gang nervous. If the Germans had made the capture, it seemed that they'd be likely to come on through after us. Thrasher spent the morning rounding up a few mules for us. At one o'clock a messenger arrived from Shepr. We immediately questioned him about Gary, but had seen nothing of him and knew no more than we did. The note he carried directed us on to another village and we lost no time getting under way.

Once more we were on our own, although we hoped and expected to keep contact with the British. We missed Gary, his easy confidence, his experience, his rugged, hard-boiled way of meeting whatever situation that confronts us. Now he was gone, and we added this loss to the score we had to settle with the Jerries.

By mule-back and on foot we pushed along the trail for two hours and then halted for a rest and some smokes. While we were engaged in rolling our cigarettes, getting them going, and beginning to talk again about our prospects and plans, the sharp eyes of Bill Eldridge spotted a brand new pair of gloves lying a couple of feet off the trail just opposite to where he was sitting. Bill got up lazily, sauntered over and picked them up.

"Thank you, Santa Claus," he grinned, as he came back.

"Boy," said Adams, "you're the luckiest fool alive."

"He's a live fool and we're the lucky ones," Cranson declared. "What if that been a booby trap? Blown us all to kingdom come! Gary would skin you alive for picking up stuff like that. Let's see them. I think those will just about fit me."

Bill blew a long streamer of smoke. Then he threw back his head and gave a good imitation of the tobacco auctioneer on the Lucky Strike program, winding it up with "sold to American."

"And I'm the American," he added, his eyes mocking Cranson. Meanwhile Paul Allen was working on the idea that where there was one pair of gloves there might be two, prowling the edge of the trail.

"Somebody's pack sprung a leak," he said, showing us several rifle cartridges he had picked up. "Can't wear them, can't eat them, can't even shoot them," he mourned.

"Give them to me," Owen suggested, "I'll trade them for some medicine, next town we hit."

"Why, doctor," Paul grinned, shoving the cartridges into his pocket, "I believe you got something there."

Everybody had their guess as to how the gloves and cartridges were there on the trail, but Paul's ideas that they had dropped from someone's pack was most logical.

"Maybe they belong to some one in our brigade," one of the girls said, with a laugh.

The "brigade" was, according to information given us by Steffa, a battalion of patriot soldiers whose duty it was to keep between us and the enemy at all times. We had never seen them, and they were, so far as we were concerned, a mythical outfit, counted largely as existing only in the imagination of Steffa. We could always depend on the "brigade," he assured us, and as long as the "brigade" was with us there would be no surprise from the enemy. Steffa served us well, perhaps better than we know, but we were never quite sure when to believe him.

December 17, 1943, Friday – To Progonat

On our way again, we hiked for another hour and then came to a small, burned-out village where the people gave us some cornbread and raw onions. We washed the food down the water from village well. After a conference with Steffa and some of the townsmen, C.B. told us that the next town was under Barley control and that he and Baggs, with Steffa, would go on ahead of the main party to scout things out a little. We were to follow them at an interval of about thirty minutes.

We waited the appointed time and then set out. Somehow, someway, whether by design of someone in the column or just by a combination of circumstances, we worked ourselves into a state of great hilarity as we struggled along the trail. No raki in it. At least I didn't see any. It was just one of those times when everything we did or said was funny. We were tired and hungry, and many were weakened by further attacks of dysentery, but all joined in the fun. Over and over we sang "Role on Mule," yelling and laughing and having a great time. About thirty minutes out, I had to make a side trip and fell behind the gang. They sent one of the native guides back after me and when I rejoined I was promptly put on a mule. Bob Owen was also riding, and farther ahead in the column I could see Lt. Jean Rutkowski bobbing up and down to the pace of her mount.

The singing, yelling and cutting up was still going on. Paul Allen picked up a stout switch, sneaked carefully up to Owen's mule, and then, with a wild howl that was out of this world, gave the beast a stinging larrup across the rump. The startled animal lurched into a lumbering trot and Bob kicked and yelled my mule into action as he went by. Rutkowski pummeled her mule into a trot to join us and for the next few minutes we went completely foolish. First we were cowboys, riding the range in pursuit of a band of rustlers; then we were jockeys, rising in the Kentucky Derby. Through it all we whooped, laughed, and dug our heels into the mules. The little animals switched their tails and shook their heads as if in protest, but most of the time we kept them at a trot that was slightly faster than the pace set by the foot troops. Before long; however, we came to a section of trail that was too steep and rugged for riding and were forced to dismount and lead our mules up to the summit.

Most of the mules were lazy and took plenty of urging over places like this. Owen's mue, as if to repay him for the extra workout, simply balked at this point and wouldn't move a step. Bob tugged and roared at the beast while we all shouted encouragement and advice, none of which he appreciated or followed. He finally resorted to use of a stick he picked up and even pelted the animal with rocks. But there it stood. We moved on ahead. Looking back from a hundred yards or so, I saw Bob give the mule an angry kick. Then he began to yell.

"Come on back here and get your damned mule," he shouted. "I'm done with him. Come on get him! If I had my gun I'd shoot the damn stubborn beast! Nothing but crow bait anyhow!"

We were still laughing when Bob came stamping into the file, plenty sore about the whole thing. But by the time we topped out on the mountain and could again mount our steeds, his anger had passed and we continued, a very light-hearted party, into the village.

Thrasher, Baggs, and Steffa met us in a dingy old barroom. They had quarters arranged for us and we were all soon settled for the night.

December 18, 1943, Saturday – 9:00 a.m. - To Progonat

At nine the next morning, while we loafed around the village square, waiting for the mules to be packed, I heard somebody yell, "Hey! Look who's coming to town!"

It was Gary and Blondie. We gave them a rousing welcome, overjoyed to know that our fears of their capture were unfounded. We all expected some sort of explanation from Gary, but not a word did he say so far as I heard then or ever. What held them up, unless, as someone had suggested, they were, "having themselves a time," none of our enlisted bunch ever knew. Gary simply took hold and went right on as if he'd never been missing and counted as captured or dead. This time we pulled out with Gary in the lead again, leaving C.B., Baggs and Steffa back in the village, promising to come on later. We never knew the reason for this arrangement either. But we'd been in the army long enough not to ask. We just pushed on out of town.

We were all on foot, the mules having been left with the leaders. But the way led down grade. It was cold, although not low enough to freeze the mud in the trail. With our shoes in bad shape that would have been tough. The sky was overcast with a blanket of gray clouds, promising rain or snow, though none was falling yet. The air was raw and sharp, but as long as we kept moving we were fairly comfortable, except for our feet, always wet, cold and sore.

We plugged along until a stream barred our way. It was not too deep and some of the nurses and enlisted men took off their shoes and socks, rolled up pant legs, and waded through the icy water. The less hardy ones walked up and down the bank, looking for a better way to cross and were soon rewarded by the appearance of an Albanian farmer with a couple of mules. Gary commandeered the animals and within a short time we were all assembled and moving on again. An hour later, while we stopped in a small village, an old woman came out of one of the houses with two strings of figs and went around giving some to each of us. Nurse Nelson busied herself here by filling canteens for everybody.

"You know," Cruise philosophized as he chewed his figs, "it takes all kinds of people to make Albania; the same as it does any other place. Some say to hell with you and let it go at that. Then there are others, like this old lady now, who go out of their way to be as nice as they can to us. Yes sir, you sure do run into all kinds of people."

From here the trail swung sharply upward again and we were soon panting and struggling up another of those endless mountains. Every time we hit the up trail now we were thinking that it had to be our last; we couldn't keep on forever, climbing mountains and plodding down the other side. Yes, we knew the Germans were in the valleys, that we had to keep to the high ground as much as possible, but day by day our condition was going down hill, and we knew it. Gary led and urged us along for two hours, bringing us into Golem, where he called a halt at last. We met the council president and Gary asked him for cornbread, but none was available. Golem had been burned, almost totally destroyed. We pushed wearily on.

Half an hour went by and it was noticed that one of our nurses, Lt. Jensen, was missing. Gary set out immediately over the back trail. Before long we saw him coming along the trail gain with the attractive young Michigan girl mounted on the mule beside him. We looked at Jensen as they came up. She looked back and tried to smile, but was too weak to make much of it. No questions were needed. We simply started on again. We didn't even ask Gary where he'd got the mule. While we had been waiting, two of the girls had thrown away their battered and worn out galoshes. Lt. Nelson, our South Carolinian, voiced the thoughts of the party when she said, "Gary's a good guy; he wouldn't leave anybody behind."

We continued on into the village of Progonat, another place ravaged by fire, although a number of the houses remained in fair condition. It was five o'clock and darkness was closing in when we got there. The town leader took us into a store and Gary bought some wine that was good and seemed to give us the lift we so badly needed. Quarters were arranged and before we left Gary gave each group of five another bottle of wine.

December 19, 1943, Sunday – 10:00 a.m. - Progonat

The next day we assembled at the store and around ten o'clock Thrasher, Baggs and Steffa came in. We waited, expecting word to get under way, but none came. Then we learned that the Jerries were operating in a valley about two hours away. Before noon a Nazi fighter plane appeared, and, from our perch well up on the mountain, we could watch its movements as it strafed the distant valley. The grumble of artillery and mortar fire became plainly audible, and more German fighters appeared.

"And that isn't an Albanian wedding," Lebo announced, his eyes fixed on the ridge that hid the battle from us.

At noon Thrasher called us together to say that we would remain in the village over night, hoping that the Germans would carry out their usual tactics of plunder and retreat.

We went to our billets, a pretty glum crowd. Our spirits, so high only the day before, were again very low. The long weeks of mountain climbing, the inadequate food, clothing and shoes totally insufficient to withstand the winter weather that was closing in, the continued attacks of dysentery, all combined to bring us to the edge of despair.

Bob Owen, going to the privy this night, was attacked by a vicious dog belonging to our host. In his effort to escape, slipped and fell. The huge beast leaped for Bob's throat with a savage snarl and I believe would have killed the New Yorker before aid could have reached him if Owen had not flung out his hand in an instinctive gesture of defense. The dog's jaw closed on it. Two Albanians, hearing the scuffle, poured out of the house, yelling, but by this time Bob had managed to get loose and was on his feet, picking them up and laying them down, with the dog nipping at his heels. He dashed between the two natives, nearly spilling one, and made the house. The hand was torn, but did not seem to be deeply injured. We fixed him up as best we could with the stuff we had with us. It was just one more thing to add to the blue funk we were in.

December 20 1943, Monday – 8:00 a.m. - Progonat

At eight o'clock in the morning we went down to the store to see what was doing; and an hour later Gary and Blondie moved out as a reconnaissance party to see if they could check on the position of the Germans. C.B. bought us some figs and a few oranges to serve as breakfast and we followed the British at an interval of an hour. At eleven a rabble of Italian and Albanian refugees came pouring down the trail into us and we learned that they were evacuating a village a few hours away. It didn't look too good for our getting through. Jim Cruise tramped up and down in the mud, paying no heed to the efforts at conversation that were being made.

"Nuts!" we heard him muttering, "nuts! Oh, hell! Dam the luck! Nuts!"

We decided to push on in spite of the disturbing news. But we had hardly more than started when up ahead we saw Gary and Blondie with a third British, hustling toward us, while behind them the trail seems to be filled with Albanian soldiers. Steffa stood still among us, his eyes fixed on the approaching column.

"The brigade," he muttered to those nearest him, "that's our brigade."

After that we stood in silence, except for the rumble of guns beyond the shoulder of the mountain. We knew the news was bad and at the moment we were almost past caring how bad it was. Gary's face, as he came up, was as glum as any of ours.

"A big push," we heard him say to Thrasher and Baggs. "They're kicking bloody hell out of the Albanians. There are dead everywhere. Not a mouse could get through those Jerry lines now. This non-com of ours had to make a bally run for it without a scrap of his gear."

So there it was. This was the k-o for us. The Huns had us stopped. We weren't getting out. We were washed up. We could climb mountains on our hands and knees, we'd done it; we could live on cornbread and sour milk, we'd done that; we could sleep with the lice and fleas chewing us, march in the rain and go barefoot if we had to. All these things we could do, while there was ahead of us the hope of the blue sea, the hope of getting back to our lines, the hope of home! Now that hope was gone. We knew we were too far done to go back. There was nothing left in us that said, "Keep on." It was the 20th of December, forty three days after our landing. We'd made a good fight of it, but, the fight was over.

13 – High Hopes Brought Low

December 20, 1943, Monday – Leaving Progonat

I think the word "surrender" was in the mind of every one of us. But no one was willing to voice the thought. We had no wish for talking anyway. It was even hard for us to meet the eyes of our comrades, knowing that every glance must betray the hopelessness we felt. Gary rallied us.

"Come on, chaps," he said, gruffly, "We can't stand here and let the bally push roll back on us. Here we go."

We followed him, numb to everything but the fact that we were turning back. We'd done a lot of wandering around, much of that time we'd been certain it was aimless, but this was the first time we'd been stopped, our route completely cut off. Along the way, Jock, the British sergeant, who had pulled out of the battle zone without equipment or clothing, save for the stuff he was wearing, spoke to our native guide, Pandee.

"Why don't you sing?" Jock asked. "You should be happy. You are in your own country, among your own friends."

Pandee looked at the British soldier, but made no answer. We watched him as he hurried on ahead to confer with another of our Albanians. It took a little time for us to see that Jock's words were cruel and thoughtless. We were thinking of the battle only in terms of our own disappointment. Pandee, of course, had friends, relatives, perhaps even members of his family, who were being slaughtered up there by the Germans. We marched in on morose silence, inwardly cursing Adolph Hitler and all Nazis with every step we took. All our trials, our dangers, our escapes, were nothing compared with this one blow that seemed utterly final. It was our blackest hour.

Gary, Blondie and Jock left us before long, taking the trail back in Progonat, where they planned to spend the night and try to contact Cairo. We were to go on to Kalonja by way of Golem. As the Englishmen strode away, Thrasher called after them,

"Tell them they've got to send a plane in after us now!"

Gary made no answer. But the words came as a shaft of light in black darkness for us. "They've got to send a plane," we told ourselves. And we began to feel a little better. We marched into Golem again at three o'clock and encountered another group of retreating patriots among who were some women soldiers. One of the girls could speak very good English and told us her father was living in New York. We stayed in town a couple of hours while C.B. talked with the patriot commander. During the conference he called us all in and asked our opinion on the idea of returning to Argyrokastron and waiting for a plane to pick us up at the abandoned airport. The Albanian leader had informed him that the field was not mined, as so many such places were. Anything that carried a glimmer of hope sounded good then. We said we thought it was a swell idea, not even caring to ask Thrasher how he knew there was going to be a plane. We had little food and then, as dusk was falling, we took off for Kalonja, leaving C.B., Baggs and Steffa in Golem to spend the night and follow on next morning, going around by Progonat in hopes of getting information on the air field to Cairo.

Darkness fell soon after we were on the trail, but we hustled along all we could because a storm threatened. By the time we entered Kalonja rain was falling steadily and we were wet and cold. The town was full of patriot soldiers. I was plugging along in the dark, thinking I was with our group, when I suddenly realized that we were on the outskirts of the village.

"Hey, you birds," I yelled, "Isn't this where we hole up for tonight?"

From the darkness came a deep voiced laugh. Then men crowded around me, jabbering in Albanian. The only words I understood were an occasional "Americano." I realized that I'd gotten mixed up with a bunch of patriots who were either heading for the battle or hauling their tails out of it; I didn't know or care which. While I was fumbling around for a way to tell them I wanted to back to my group, I felt somebody grab me by the sleeve and give a tug. I took the words he said to mean "come along," and down the trail, through the blackness, we went a dog trot. Back in town my companion asked a question with "Americano" in it of everyone we met and received a reply in Albanian. After about twenty minutes he brought me up in front of a house where there was a light. More Albanians passed between my patriot and the man of the house. At about the third "Americano" a girl's voice from inside the dwelling called,

"What's the trouble?"

"Sergeant Abbott reporting," I yelled in my best military manner, "how's chances to speak some Americano around here?"

"Oh, it's you, Orville," said Lt. Jensen, coming to the door. "What's the matter? Is anything wrong?

"Not now," I said. "I just go mixed up with a column of patriots and when I woke up we were out in the rural district. They all look alike in the dark. Can you tell me how to get to our billet?"

Jensen told me that some of the enlisted men were at the next house down the road, so I paddled off through the rain. My Albanian rescuer had disappeared as soon as the nurse came to the door. Outside of giving him a communist salute I couldn't have known how to thank him, anyway.

The boys gave me the raspberries when I stumbled in.

"Ah, Mr. Abbott I presume," began Cruise in lofty fashion, but Paul Allen cut him off.

"Where you been?" he demanded. "Don't you know there is a war on?"

"Let him tell his story," Owen urged. "It'll be good."

"He loves to go walking in the rain," Cruise chanted. "Old rain in the face Abbott!"

"Well," I said, and stopped short, looking at them. "Aw, can it. What you got to eat?"

Cruise leaped to his feet, thrust his fingers into his hair, and screamed at the top of his voice, "Cornbread!"

"Wish I'd kept going," I said. But Jim had given us a laugh and for that night, a laugh was something.

Through the long hours of darkness we could hear the sodden thresh of the rain outdoors, damp chills from it penetrated the room and the blankets we had, keeping us shivering and wakeful.

December 21, 1943, Tuesday morning - Kalonja

Gray day light brought no let up in the storm. The whole world dripped, and the two men who went out to find what word there was for the day were soaked from head to foot, traveling through the mud and puddles of rain. They came back cold and discouraged, but brought orders for us to stay holed up for the day. Our two pilots, Steffa, and the three British had passed through Progonat early in the morning, leaving us a little food. They were going on to another village to make plans for our future moves, the messengers told us.

"Future hell," growled Allen, rubbing his hands slowly as he squatted by the fire, "there isn't any future in this. One village is about as good as the next, far as I can see. This is a right guy we're staying with here. I'm planning to stay with him. He hasn't much to eat. Maybe I'll end up nothing but a pile of bones. But I won't be doing any more of this GD walking."

We stared at the big, unshaven Kentuckian. Paul wasn't kidding. He didn't crack the ghost of a grin, or shift his eyes from the fire. It seemed that we couldn't summon the strength to argue with him. We all felt pretty much as he did. There were no arguments we could make. None of us believe we had a chance. We didn't know what we were to do. All we could think of was that we were through. It was Sgt. Bill Eldridge, barging in at our door, who broke the spell that had gripped us.

"HI, you bunch of flea bitten, buzzard baits," he yelled genially, "Is this the headquarters of the Albanian louse carrier command?"

"Where'd you get it?" growled Owen.

"A very small bottle," Bill declared, "strictly one portion, you understand; but very high class, really superior."

Bill had spent the night in what remained of a burned out dwelling. He had an eye for places like that, always going over them carefully for nooks and crannies that might contain material of interest to him. In this case his search had been rewarded by a bottle of raki, apparently accounting for his comparatively high spirits.

We dragged through the day, checking the weather every few minutes, some playing a half hearted game of poker, other moping. Now and then a little flare of talk would spring up about getting home, but we couldn't carry it, it wouldn't build for us.

A bunch of us went up to the village water hole at noon. There we found some of the nurses gathered around the big stone basin into which the water flowed. They were busy washing clothes. They too were restless, wanting to do something, not caring much what it was as long as it kept them occupied. All through the day, heavy gray clouds scudded along overhead, with the ceiling very low, and there were occasional showers.

December 22, 1943, Wednesday morning – Leaving Kalonja

The next morning brought no improvement in the weather. While we waited at the assembly point, on orders from our leaders, the rain came down and drenched us. At last we got started, Owen, Shumway and I in the vanguard. Within a few minutes there were shouts and calls from behind, telling us we'd taken the wrong trail. So our plan to set the pace went sour. We got going again in the mud and rain and stumbled into the village where our officers were waiting. We stopped only long enough to roll a few smokes and then pushed on down the side of the mountain. Squalls of cold rain swept in gray sheets down the valley as we marched across it. We all kept moving. No one was willing to be the first to drop out. We simply kept putting one foot ahead of the other. The going was bad and our morale was the lowest it had been. Mud seeped up through our tattered shoes and caked in hard little balls under our toes, bringing a painful pressure that sent offshoots through the whole foot. At last we came to a stream where some of the group had halted and were filling canteens. A few had crusts of bread they were nibbling on while others were busy with tobacco and papers.

"The Jerries even have the weather working for them," Lebo complained dully. He stood under a tree, hunched over to keep the wet off the cigarette he was rolling.

Most of the crowd was silent. Everybody flopped down in the wet, eager to give aching feet a moment's respite. Only our officers knew the results of the urgent radio message sent via Cairo to General Carl Andrew Spaatz, then commanding the Fifteenth Air Force and Royal Air Forces in Italy. But we didn't have to ask. A glance at Thrasher's face told us there was no good news from that quarter.

"What are we going to do, Orville?" Jim Cruise asked, as we squatted beside the trail. "There's no percentage in this."

"Can't buck city hall," I agreed, and rubbed my dripping nose with the back of my hand. It seemed then that stumbling into a German patrol and being taken prisoner wouldn't be the worst thing that could happen to us. But we got going again, struck a main traveled road and soon crossed a bridge over a large stream. After that we took to trails again, working away from the road. In an hour we came to a burned out village where we chiseled some green onions from the natives. This was the only food we had on that hike. In this place we saw several bee hives. Sgt. Eldridge eyed them with longing but was unable to get a campaign for acquiring some of the contents worked up during the short stop we made. A mile or so out of town was again barred by a large river, possibly the same one we had previously crossed. We ferried it in an old scow manned by an Albanian, but it held us up for an hour. At the next village the officers and nurses were billeted for the night and we enlisted men proceeded to another place about thirty minutes away.

On our arrival we were taken to the village council house and into a room where two big fires had been built. We began stripping out of our wet clothes and stringing them around to dry. Just getting in out of the weather and knowing that for the time being we were through with walking in the mud meant the difference between heaven and earth to us that night. We sat around soaking up the heat from those fires and even managed a few feeble wisecracks. Supper, when it was ready, was the biggest and most pleasant surprise we'd had in many a day. That meal was served on a long table and each one of us had a chair to sit in while he ate. There was even a white table cloth on that table.

"Fellas," Jim Cruise began in solemn wonder, "we're all dead and gone to heaven! This is pretty near like home!"

Jim's voice wavered a little on the last words and he looked down quickly to hide the tears that came unexpectedly to his eyes. Jim was trying to laugh. He didn't get it, but he had spoken very close to the feelings of all of us, then came the supper. Great Lord! We had lamb and chicken on that table. There were steaming bowls of rice soup. Even the cornbread tasted good.

"This isn't a meal," Lebo declared, shaking his hand, "it's a banquet!"

Paul Allen looked up from the plate he was scraping.

"Chow for a king," he agreed. "Damn if I am not glad I didn't stay with that old bachelor after all. Been wishing all day I'd done it, but I'm feeling better."

The luck held. We were billeted that night in twos and threes and every one of us had a mattress to sleep on!

December 23, 1943, Thursday – morning - Karla

The warmth, the good people, the food and a good night's rest did wonders for us and when we returned to the council house the next morning our spirits were returning to normal. Hanging outside on the porch was a huge bunch of dried onions. The people gave us some, but I have to record that we also hooked some for ourselves. We did it while Sgt. Hayes was trying out some of the Italian he had learned in conversation with the Albanian who could speak it. By the time we sat down to breakfast our pockets were bulging with dried onions, but the Albanians seem to be willing to overlook this breach of hospitality on our part. When it comes to food and other things considered necessities, people situated as we were lose all understanding of that Bible verse that says something about things being given to those that have and taken away from those that have not. We operated on the reverse of that idea, but at this place restrained our "salvaging" operations strictly to dried onions. The "inner voice" of each of us had become pretty well toughened to such things in our weeks of wandering, but the treatment received at this place was too good to allow our operations to become extensive.

December 23, 1943, Thursday – 5:00 p.m. - Arrive in Doksat

We moved down the trail to the village hosting the rest of our party very slowly that morning because Bob Owen was bare footed.

When we got to the assembly point Bob was put on a mule and so, we carried on. A two-hour hike brought us into a village where we stopped for dinner and then we moved on to a place called Doksat, arriving about five o'clock on the night of December 23. Once more the party was split up and we enlisted men were sent on to Kesovrat. Both of these towns were directly across the valley from Argyrokastron, where the abandoned airport was located, and a journey of about two hours.

At Kesovrat, some of the Albanians had butchered sheep and hogs for their Christmas feasts and we fared very well.

December 24, 1943, Friday – Doksat and Kesovrat

The next day we loafed around the council room, where fires burned on the big hearths. There were some English speaking Albanians here. One man came in with the greeting, "Hi there, partners!" and then went around the room shaking hands with each of us and offering us tailor made cigarettes which we gladly accepted. After a time we were all taken to a large house. Our room; however, was quite small for our number, but a fire was going and we made the best of it. Supper was served in an adjoining room, banquet style again, and the food was good, but there wasn't enough of it this time. When we got back to our room we found that a spark from our fire had set the rug to smoldering. The commotion we made putting it out summoned the old dame of the house who started in on us with an angry torrent of Albanian. But Jim Cruise was ready with a counter attack.

"Why, grandma!" he yelled back, with a big Irish smile, "How you talk!" He advanced with out stretched arms and folded the old girl into a fond embrace. She struggled and sputtered while Cruise kissed her jovially on both cheeks and patted her shoulder. We cheered and whistled. Johnny Wolf leaped forward to back Jim with secondary support, landing a kiss on her forehead and slipping an arm around her shoulders. The route was complete, "grandma" fled with skirts flying. But she's stopped the rush of angry Albanian. Cruise rubbed his hands briskly and then held them out to the fire.

"You always got to kiss a woman when she's mad," he observed blandly.

"The hell you say," put in Bob Owen, "last time I tried it I got my ears beat down and was damn near thrown in the brig!"

"Not enough Irish," drawled Jim, amid the laughter, "not enough Irish, me boy."

"All right, all right," Owen said, with deep sarcasm, "do your crowing while the crowing is good. That old gal's probably gone out to get the brigade to come clean house on us." But we did not see or hear anything further from our hostess.

A man named John was hired to do our cooking for us and the president of the village took over the job of procuring the food. We spent the day before Christmas in our rather cramped quarters, playing cards and sitting around on the floor sewing tears in our clothes with surgical sutures and needles. Some of the boys sent their shoes to a cobbler in hopes of getting them repaired. We drew lots to see who would go down to the other village to contact our commanders. But the two who were finally stuck with the trip brought back nothing new.

It was Christmas Eve. Supper was spread for us by lamp light in the larger room. We moved in slowly. On this night the first men in stood behind their chairs and waited. Nobody had much to say. Then from somewhere down the table came a voice.

"Somebody ought to offer a prayer tonight."

"Won't make the chow go any further, will it?" another questioned.

"No, but it's Christmas Eve and it isn't going to do us any harm. We have to do something for Christmas."

"Maybe you got something there."

"Come on, Orville. You're ranking non-com."

I looked around the table, at their faces, trying to make sure this wasn't a rib they were putting on me. No grins were being hidden. They were simply waiting for me. I stepped back to see the light, taking from my pocket the little prayer book that was with me then and will be with me always.

"Bless us, O Lord," I read, "and these thy gifts, which we are about to receive from Thy bounty. And be Thou the eternal food for our souls, through Christ our Lord. Amen."

We all sat down and began to eat. The food was fair, but again there wasn't enough of it. When we had cleaned up everything in sight we were still hungry. Cruise pushed back his bowl and rested his arms on the table.

"Read us some more from that book, Reverend," he said, and smiled, but there was no derision in his eyes. I know that many of the boys were carrying prayer books and that some kept up with their prayers night and morning and that others of the boys who didn't have books also prayed. So much of the time these last few days there seemed nothing left for us to do, but to keep on praying that somehow we'd make it and get back to our lines. Once more I took out my book.

"We give Thee thanks, O Almighty God, for all Thy benefits, who livest and reignest now and forever. Amen. May the souls of the faithful departed, through the mercy of God, rest in peace. Amen. Visit, we beseech Thee, O Lord, this place, and drive far from it all the snares of the enemy. May Thy Holy Angels dwell here in to keep us in peace, and may Thy blessing be on us always. Amen."

The fellows got up slowly and we trooped back into our small room in complete silence. There, Paul Allen and a few others began cracking some nuts, the sound of the popping shells coming loud in the quiet. Soon though, the boys began to talk, in low tones; short sentences punctuated by long silences. We had a bottle or two of wine, which passed from hand to hand. The talk gradually became more general, all of it about home and Christmas. Somebody began to hum a Christmas carol. Zieber picked up the words in his tuneful baritone and we all joined in. Another was suggested and sung. Then Zieber hummed softly the first bars of "Silent Night."

"Can that," somebody protested, "They'll be taking us for a bunch of Germans!"

Zieber stopped. For just a moment his gaze shifted from face to face around the circle.

"To hell with them!" he said distinctly. Then he began to sing, "Silent night, Holy night! All is calm, all is bright!"

I could feel the tears on my cheeks, and didn't try to stop them.

14 – Germans Cut Off Air Rescue

December 25, 1943, Saturday - Christmas in Doksat

"Merry Christmas, rise and shine, you bunch of lugs! Merry Christmas!" were the holiday greetings from those who were awake to those who were taking their turn at sleeping. Our room was so small that only part of us could stretch out on the floor at a time. Now, the dim light of Christmas dawn was in the room and the boys were stirring. For a few minutes the holiday spirit took hold of us. We shook hands, slapped shoulders, did a lot of yelling, got in some wisecracks, and laughed a lot. Then, as was inevitable, somebody began talking about spending the next Christmas day at home. The damper went down. We were ragged, tired, hungry, lousy, unshaven and dirty. Not enough tobacco in the crowd to roll a cigarette apiece. But what we had we shared in the true spirit of Christmas. When Christmas dinner was served, I was called on again for prayers.

After dinner Hornsby and Allen made the trip to the other village to confer with Thrasher and find out if there was anything new. When they came back they brought some Christmas with them. The British had radioed for supplies and our two liaison men were laden with articles of clothing that had been dropped from the planes. In the pile of stuff were four pairs of long wool socks, two pairs of pants, three jackets, three gas proof suits, several suits of underwear and a pair of boots. The boots didn't fit Owen, who was most in need of them, but were right for Shumway, who was going through the flying boots he'd been wearing. Hornsby, Wolf and I got the jackets. I think Lebo and MacKinnon got the pants. The rest was passed around where it was most needed and would fit. Some of the stuff was made in Philadelphia, Pa., so we were getting some of our lend lease.

The patriots presented us with a live sheep and Johnny Wolf and the Albanian who had greeted us as "partners" did the butchering. But that animal didn't expand our menu that day. The dinner was cornbread and goat soup and for supper our appetites were tickled with fried onions and some lettuce. After supper Bill Eldridge left the room on tiptoe and returned as quietly a minute later with a fat round log over his shoulder. He laid it gently on our fire.

"Our Yule log?" questioned Owen, sardonically.

"That's right," grinned Bill, "and I stole it."

"God bless ye, me boy!" exclaimed Cruise heartily, and we all had a laugh.

So it was Christmas night, and as men folk will, we sat around our Yule log, telling and listening to fantastic tales of life before the war. MacKinnon was a forest ranger and we razzed him on his mountain climbing after hearing his story. Paul Allen, by his own account, had been everything from a truck driver to a newspaper reporter. Lebo and Adams were former railroad men and proved it by giving us some good yarns. A railroad man can always come up with a story. We sat late around the fire and then began our sleeping shifts.

December 26, 1943, Sunday - Doksat

Morning brought the day after Christmas and the loss of our brotherly love and comradeship. We were convinced that we were well on the way to starving to death in this place. Tempers and nerves went on edge overnight and we acted like a bunch of mountain pirates. We simply scraped bottom on tobacco. A cigarette being rolled called for immediate and concentrated attention from everybody. About ten men would call butts on a smoke that not more than six could get a drag from, and this of course led to arguments that rankled more or less. Some of us had saved a few coins and pooled the money to buy some food. We gave it to Allen with instructions to come back with something to eat. Paul came back with an armful of cornbread! When we gave him hell for being so slow about it, he explained that the man he bought it from insisted that he sit down and have a cup of coffee with him before closing the deal. Then he went after him for throwing our money away on cornbread and he hauled a hard boiled egg out of his pocket and began telling us how he had finally made the man include it in the deal.

We cleaned up the cornbread and our egg, a thirteenth share to each man, and it did us no good. Then the tobacco shortage reached a climax when two of the boys started swinging fists over whose turn it was on a butt. For a while we just sat still and watched them, not caring whether anybody got hurt or not. It didn't seem important what happened to us. Then Lebo got up and parted the scrappers. Their little exertion had exhausted them and when Lebo went between them, one of the boys fell down. The peacemaker then tried to get them to shake hands, but they wouldn't do it. We had a miserable evening, sitting around our tiny room, waiting, worrying, and not knowing why we were held up in this place; killing off what little hope we had, trying to school ourselves for the worst.

That night, while part of the bunch was sleeping, Bill Eldridge made a foray into the matron's pantry and came back with corn meal and olive oil, mixing a batter in his mess kit and baking it over the fire. Bill had eyed the place carefully during our stay and there was not a nook or cranny in it that he didn't know. He later salvaged some quinces the lady had put in what she thought was safe place. I'll bet there was some fast Albanian with "Americano" in it when she found they were gone. I'd like to have seen Cruise kiss her out of that.

December 27, 1943, Monday - Doksat

About eight o'clock next morning, after some of us had made a skimpy breakfast and others, on the late sleeping shift, were beginning to stretch and growl, Lebo declared he heard machine gun fire.

"A window rattling," I said, "you're nerves are shot."

"The hell they are," Lebo flared back, "I know machine gun fire when I hear it!"

I'd spoken more in an attempt to quiet some of the fellows who'd begun to scramble around for their shoes and make ready for a hasty departure. Some were putting on shoes for the first time in four days. What little sole leather we had left was really horded.

Within ten minutes we could plainly hear artillery and mortar fire from the valley but could not see where it was landing or guess what the disturbance was about. We finished our breakfast, got our stuff together and then waited impatiently for word from our commanders. We rather expected to see the whole party come pouring in with the Germans on their heels. But nobody appeared and no word came. Finally two of the boys set off for the village that housed the officers and nurses, planning to bring back whatever news they could pick up. We waited and grumbled, listening to the firing as we moved about restlessly.

It had been raining steadily for a week, but on this morning a break had come in the clouds so that now and then some pale sunshine came through. Our two messengers were back in little more than an hour.

"The Jerries are kicking the hell out of Argyrokastron," they reported.

"There goes our airfield!" Cruise concluded, gloomily.

"Not yet," said one of the boys who had made the trip. "But they are sure giving the town a going over. The dope C.B. has from his Albanian recognizance is that this bunch of Nazis is a panzer column moving up from somewhere in Greece. They had a small patrol on motor bikes out in front and when they came into sight of Argyrokastron about dark last night some damn fool patriot threw a grenade into them. So they stopped long enough to mop up, just our damned luck!"

"So what?" somebody wanted to know. "They'll stay on the main road. We don't have to worry."

"That's what you think!" someone answered pointedly. "That grenade fouled things to hell for us; that's all. Last night C.B. and they figured the weather was going to break. So they shoot a message into Cairo again for plans to take us out. They think a squadron is coming in. So now all we have to do is sit here on our rear ends, and play 'eni, meeni, meini and mo' to find out if the Jerries pull out or planes get here first. And all because some Albanian gets hot and slings a grenade. Wish it had blown him to hell before he let it loose! The Patriots C.B. talked to claim the Germans would've moved right on through except for that, and we'd been sitting pretty."

We took the news in stunned silence.

"What's Thrasher say we're to do?" somebody asked finally.

"We lay low until they can find out more about what the Jerries are doing. If they move on, everything is O.K. If they don't then I don't know. Anyway, we're waiting for orders."

Bob Owen rubbed his grimy hands between his knees thoughtfully. His eyes reflected the picture that was in all our minds; the picture of American transports coming in to land, coming in for us, coming to take us home! It was wonderful, beautiful. It had to come true.

"Boys," Bob said slowly, "if those planes touch wheel to ground I am to get on. There aren't enough Jerries in Albania to keep me from trying it anyhow."

We were with him to a man. This would be the show down for us. We were at the end of the rope. Right then we felt as if we didn't care to go on living unless we could get on one of those transports. We were convinced it was our last chance, our one and only hope of getting out. We talked about nothing else all that day, each of us trying to key up the courage of the group to a point of desperation, each bolstering their own determination. After going through that day I think I know a little about how it feels to be in a suicide squad. Your body shrinks and chills but your mind throws back the constant attacks of doubt that would deflect it from the chosen course. So we made ourselves ready for the test. At least we thought we were ready to load transport under German fire.

However, we did not forget that there was a chance that the Germans would pull out of Argyrokastron, and we spent a lot of time outside, listening to the firing. It continued in sporadic bursts most of the day and when it finally stopped, someone immediately voiced the idea of going down and contacting Thrasher. But army discipline prevailed.

"He said to sit tight and we'd hear from him," one of the messengers pointed out.

No sooner had we decided that the firing was definitely over than we began arguments as to what might be the meaning.

"If they got orders for another place they'll pull out!"

"Nuts! Not until they eat and drink up everything they can get their hands on!"

"Gary claims there's a Gestapo man in town, or was anyhow, and that he knows we're around here somewhere. They might sit down for a week and send patrols out after us."

"Hell! They don't give a damn for us! If they'd wanted us they'd had us long ago."

So it went, up one side and down the other, for the rest of the day and far into the night.

December 28, 1943, Tuesday – Morning - Doksat

Tuesday morning we were up early and our toes, ready to take off on the instant word from Thrasher arrived. The hours dragged on to noon. The weather was still good. We talked about nothing but those rescue planes. We imagined everything. The flight had been cancelled. The orders were to pick up only the officers and nurses. Thrasher had sent us word by a native who was in the German pay and the fellow had skipped to the Nazis. A mistake had been made in locating us and the planes had gone to another place. There was no more firing, maybe the Jerries were on the move and the coast would be clear tomorrow. What if the weather didn't hold and we came up with zero ceiling in the morning?

We walked back and forth and up and down. We smoked everything we could get our hands on. We tried to play poker and threw the cards in, unable to keep our minds on the game. Noon passed and we had little to eat. By two o'clock we were practically unanimous in believing the whole thing was off, probably nothing but a bunch of hooey anyway. Those English! How did we know they talked to Cairo?

"Well, they call in their supply planes, don't they? You got on underwear off one of them."

"Yeah, but they won't call any planes for us. They want his majesty's army and navy to have all the publicity for getting us out."

"Well, let them have it, only by God I wish they'd produce!"

Hungry, fretful, worried, we watched the sun go down and prepared for another miserable night. I don't think anybody did more than doze, and the room was about as cheery and peaceful as a den occupied by a dozen strange wildcats when day broke at last. Through the night we had watched the weather constantly and now the sunrise seemed to portend another clear day with plenty of visibility.

December 29, 1943, Wednesday – Leaving Doksat

With daylight too, came a patriot with a note from Thrasher. Cranson took it, opened the paper and read it while we crowded around. All it said was for us to report in the lower village at 9 o'clock. But that was enough for us. It meant the planes were coming. Our spirits went up a thousand per cent. In that moment, every one of us was a hell of a good fellow, and the best friends in the world. Even our thin breakfast was made a joke.

"The sample was very good, John," we told our native cook, who understood nothing but our grins. "Sorry we can't wait for the real thing."

Off we went down the trail at a brisk dog trot, but we were soon forced to pull up, puffing and staggering. We were weaker than we'd realized. But we pushed on as fast as we could, yelling to everybody to "stick together." Reaching the village, we went at once to the officer's quarters where we found Thrasher, Baggs, the Englishmen and the nurses assembled and waiting. When we were all in the room, C.B. lit a cigarette and tried to make his announcement calmly.

"This is our D-Day," he said. "Our planes are coming over between 12 and 2. If the coast is clear, five men will run out on the field and wave their parachute panels to signal for the landing. We are all going to be hidden in the brush on the hill just beyond the air field. When the transports land we've all got to be out there ready to pile aboard. There'll be two troop carriers and I don't know what else, maybe nothing. But we'll divide the parting into two groups. Baggs will take one and I'll take the other. We'll have to guess as close as we can to where they'll stop and then hit for that place as soon as they go into their glide. The men in each group will be responsible for seeing that the nurses get through to the planes."

He blew a cloud of smoke and smiled at the girls.

"That means," he said, "that you get them there alive and no broken bones."

"Never mind the broken bones!" said Dawson, quickly.

"We leave equipment with the patriots at the air field," Thrasher went on. "Now, here's the division we've made for the two groups. If there are any objections, we can probably make some swaps. The main idea was to have them fairly equal on strength and experience."

The names were ready and nobody had any kick. The signal men named by Thrasher were Hayes, Wolf, Shumway, Lebo and me.

"One more thing," C.B. said after a moment of silence, "I'm allowed to tell you that "the old man" will be on one of the transports."

We gave a cheer at the news. That was red headed Major William P. McKnight, commander of the evacuation transport squadron, a real guy and one we'd known as boss from the very first days of our organization at Louisville, Kentucky.

"Boy!" exclaimed Owen, "you'd know Red would be right in there pitching for us! If he's on my ship I'll kiss the old bugger, moustache and all!"

We'd never been so happy. That was it. We wanted to pinch ourselves to make sure it was no dream, that in a matter of hours we'd be back and safe in Italy. We walked along the trail in the cold bright air of the morning feeling like a million bucks and chattering like a bunch of kids on the way home from school. The path led downward to the floor of a valley where we splashed through a small stream and then moved up to the brow of a hill where we caught a partial view of the village of Argyrokastron and the air field. We went on to take a position behind a low hill that offered us some brush cover and yet was only a few hundred yards from the probably landing point of the planes. There we settled down to wait, our eyes fixed on the little town where the Jerries were supposed to be, while our ears were strained to catch the first far off mutter of the engines in the rescue squadron. We waited there for a full hour, hardly moving, seldom speaking. When we did talk it was in a low voice, almost whispers, and a low, short mutter of words. Then we received the news.

"Twelve O'clock!"

About twenty minutes later we saw an Albanian come up and talk with our officers, grouped a short distance away from the hillside. Thrasher rose up and gave the assembly signal. We scurried over, closing in around him. For a minute he didn't speak, just looked around us. Then he said flatly,

"It's all off. This messenger has just left Argyrokastron. He says the Jerries have several 88's lined on the field along with tanks and other fire power waiting to blast our ships to hell as soon as they land. Gary says none of us will live to reach the ships if we try it."

We looked at Gary and he looked back at us without a waver from his dark eyes. It was suddenly very cold and bleak there on that hillside. The swift annihilation of our high hopes left us completely stunned. Bob Owen was first to recover.

"O.K.," he said grimly, "we'll take the odds. Give those of us who want to go a chance. That's all we're asking."

Gary shook his head sharply.

"Sorry," he said, quietly. "It wouldn't make the least difference if every one of us was killed, but it happens that the price in planes and the men who fly them would be too high. We can't let them land, knowing the Jerries have their guns lined on the field."

He had hardly finished speaking when one of the nurses gave a little gasp.

"Here they come," she cried, unsteadily, "Oh, here they come! They're coming! Listen! Hear them?"

We could hear them, the swiftly growing thunder of engines; many engines. We stared at the sky, mouths agape. The wild, glorious roaring of the ships grew louder and louder. Then we saw them, the bright sun flashing on their wings, wings that carried the beloved markings. We were seeing our own planes again, cheering them as they came thundering over, skimming the hilltops. Two C47 transports with the great stars blazing white on their sleek sides. A big Wellington bomber that zoomed low over the village of Argyrokastron like a bully, spoiling for a fight, daring the Jerries to open up. All around them was a protecting escort, just sauntering along at 200 or so, were two dozen P38 fighters. The transports came in and zoomed over the field with their landing gears down. A group of P38's zipped directly over our heads and we went crazy. We jumped and yelled like madmen. Fellows were clawing at Gary with tears streaming down their faces, begging him to let us give the landing signal. The C47's began swinging around the field in tight circles. Each time they made what could have been a landing run; the bomber came in with them, obviously with orders to cover the town with its guns while we loaded. Not a shot came from the Jerries in Argyrokastron.

But Gary was adamant. He refused to let us go. How even military discipline held us at that point, I don't know. We took turns watching the planes swing around the field and howling over our pleas at the sturdy British Lieutenant.

"For Christ's sake," one of the boys screamed finally, as the C47's went into their fourth circuit of the field, "they've got them bluffed! The GD Huns are in their foxholes. They are not on the guns. Those planes can land and haul before the Jerries get ready to shoot!"

Gary was wavering. Then he threw in the chips. His nod was all we needed. Behind us as we took off, we heard him yell "Cover!" as he shoved his Tommy gun at one of his sergeants. Then he was running with us. We tore our parachute scarves from our necks as we went. It was like running a 440 at the state meet. Every man of us was putting all he had into the effort of being first on that field. We were running for life or maybe death. Right then it didn't seem that we cared which. Our only thought was to stop those planes. We went two hundred yards at that pace. It was murder. Our bodies were dying, numb with the swift ebb of our strength, we had only a savage will somewhere inside that kept us going. We didn't make it.

As we neared the edge of the field the drumming clamor of the squadron was already fading into the distance. They were gone. We had lost the race. We lay flat on the ground, fighting for our breath, our hearts bursting, sobbing our despair, feeling like we were going to die and wanting to. But gradually we quieted down. Gary talked to us then. He tried to make us see that the Germans would have caught us in murderous fire. I think now that he expected them to open up if we got onto that field and that he came along to take over and get us back if he could. But right then we hated him for holding us up until we were too late. Hell! He knew when we started we couldn't make it! He was sure those plans weren't going to land.

"We'll get you blokes out," he promised, still panting from the run, "all you've got to do is stand by and carry on. The Jerries held fire while the planes were in the air because the Wellington would have blown them to hell. Besides they didn't know that our chaps knew about them being there and were waiting to shoot at sitting ducks! They'd have killed every one of you and wiped out a bomber and two transports with their crews."

We listened in sullen silence, still blaming him for the loss of this best of all chances to escape. We couldn't forgive him, but we had to admit that he probably had the dope. And Lt. Gary Duffy knew more about fighting Nazis than any ten of us. We didn't like it, but we had to give him credit for being there with us when he was sure that we were going into German fire. He could have stayed back on the hill if he'd wanted to. Gradually we got on our feet and struggled back to where the rest of the party was waiting. Jim Cruise, who had made the run with us, slammed his musette to the ground in disgust.

"Hells' bells!" he bawled, "even the day my girl and I split up I never felt as bad as this!"

From out on the field there came the noise of a sputtering exhaust. A German tank had waddled out of Argyrokastron and was strutting up and down the field in what seems to us a gesture of triumph. But it came no further and no real effort was made to capture us. If they had tried, the Germans could have rounded us up ten as easy as picking sweet corn in August. Perhaps they didn't want to be bothered with us. Right then, it didn't seem to matter much whether they were after us or not.

We dragged our way slowly back to the mountain village, the place we had hoped we would never see again. Most of us were gloomy and despondent, really on our heels. But there were stouter spirits among us.

"Weren't they beautiful?" I heard one of the girls saying. "Just to see our own planes again! It means something to know they think enough of us to send all those ships in here when it doesn't matter a penny's worth to the war whether we get out or not."

"Gary was right," a companion said. "We wouldn't want them to risk losing the two transports and that bomber just trying to pick us up. Why, oh why, did those Jerries have to sit down in that town?"

"Our luck," Jim Cruise offered, with a note of philosophical endurance, "guess we just don't live right."

Adams' voice broke the silence that followed Jim's observation.

"How those boys came in," he mused. "You'd thought they were playing tag around the old home pasture. They seemed to know every foot of the place. They must have been briefed for hours. Boy! They were really on the beam!"

Our comrades were flying a mercy mission. American Pilots and crew men, bringing their ships in to land on enemy held ground. Fighting their way in and back if need be. Would the Jerries do that? Or would the Japs? Hell, no! They'd let people like us die. It helped right then, that feeling that the American army was for us, that we meant something to the big shots. Of course, our party was different from almost any other in that we had the nurses with us. But even so, it meant that war from our side was something more than cold blooded slaughter; the sacrifice of even as small a number of troops as we were, was not simply taken for granted and forgotten. The army was willing to try for us. They'd done their best to give us a hand, get us out. It began to look as if the least we could was to keep on trying ourselves. And walking on that back trail I think we began to find the determination to do it. We were going to keep going as long as we could put one foot ahead of the other foot. And when that failed, by God we'd crawl!

15 – Bypassing German Patrols

December 29, 1943, Wednesday - Doksat

Back at the village a council was held. We couldn't quite give up the idea of getting out by plane. Army had tried once in response to our desperate message to General Spaatz, then supreme air force commander in the Mediterranean, and there was a strong feeling that we might induce them to try again. If the Germans pulled out of Argyrokastron in the next day or two; if the weather held; and if the planes could be spared, we might yet fly out of Albania. Gary had showed us the other side of the picture.

The Germans, he said, knew beyond any doubt that we were in this vicinity. They knew that the planes had come for us and that, failing this time, they might try again soon. The Jerries would be apt to wait the good weather out. They might even mine the field. All this was possible, we had to admit. So it resolved to the question of making certain what the German movements were. The conclusion was that two enlisted men would be detailed daily to go up within sight of Argyrokastron and keep close watch on the Nazis.

Gary agreed to this plan reluctantly, emphasizing the point that we could not stay much longer in the two small villages because of the drain on food supplies. Ebers and Eldridge were chosen to act as scouts for the first day. Then we enlisted men hauled out for the other village and were soon back in our little room, where food, fuel, and tempers all were short.

December 30, 1943, Thursday – Doksat

The two man detail for Argyrokastron was up and off before daylight, picking up a young Albanian to act as guide and messenger. We sweated the day out, watching the weather, holding post mortems on happenings of the day before, arguing pro and con on the question of whether we'd have another chance at the planes. It was long after dark when the two sergeants returned and they seemed surprised to find us all awake and waiting for such news as they might bring.

"Are they still there? Hell yes!" Ebers reported. "Going and coming all day long, as if they owned the place."

"They DO own it," Eldridge commented. "They left the field alone though."

The two had reported to the officers in the lower village but there was nothing new from that quarter, or at least nothing they were putting out.

"Who goes tomorrow?" someone finally asked.

"Abbott and Hornsby, and I hope they have more fun than we did. Sure is a pain."

December 31, 1943, Friday – morning - Leaving Doksat

Hornsby and I began our vigil well hidden in the brush on a hillside not far from the place where we'd made our run for the planes. We had a good view of the town and had the loan of Lt. Gary Duffy's field glasses to bring things up closer. As the previous lookouts had reported, we could see German troops, cars, trucks, and other motorized equipment moving to and from the town. Our Albanian patriot, guide and messenger, lay in a clump of brush a few feet from us. We had been there perhaps two hours when Hornsby, who was using the glasses, reached out and slapped me on the leg.

"This is it, pal," he said, in a low tone. "Jerry's got us spotted. We are not going to like this place. Let's get our eye on that jeep heading for here."

He thrust the glasses to me. I had been watching the car and had seen it turn off the main road, crossing a bridge and swinging into a lane towards the field. Now, as I brought the glasses to bear, there was the German car, moving directly towards us, three Nazis in their field grey uniforms and bucket helmets, the slim black snouts of rifles or Tommy guns sticking up beyond the shoulders of the two men who were riding. They were still several hundred yards from us and I tossed the glasses across the little space to the Albanian, motioning for him to look the car over. Hornsby and I, in the meantime, kept our eyes glued on it.

"I don't think they've spotted us," I whispered. The air was cold and crisp, and the words seemed to echo out over the valley like a shout.

"They'll blow us to hell," was Hornsby's encouraging reply.

We lay motionless on the cold ground, feeling the lice crawling over our bodies, restraining the impulse to slap and dig at them. It seemed to us then that a movement of any kind, a sneeze, a cough, would surely bring a stream of bullets from the Jerries. Not over thirty yards from our position the driver brought the car to a halt, where a footpath led out of the hill and across our front towards the town. For a full minute our popping eyes held steadily on the Germans and we hardly drew breath for fear they'd sight the tiny mist of clouds. If they killed or captured us, and we could think of no other reason for their coming out this way, no alarm would get back to the party until tonight, when we failed to show up, and that might be hours too late to save them.

Pretty soon two of the "supermen" jumped from the car and halted a native who was going along the trail to market. They exchanged a few sentences with the man and then allowed him to pass on. For twenty minutes they kept up this procedure, halting everyone who moved along the trail. Then, as suddenly as they had come, they hopped back into the car and raced off. We watched them go, relaxing the tension that had gripped us. Then we called our Albanian and told him to into the town to question the people the Germans had halted. He made his way cautiously down to the trail and set out for Argyrokastron.

Hornsby and I resumed the watch. Vehicles of the Nazi panzer division were still busy along the road. One truck I watched stopped at a farmhouse and several of the Germans got out and invaded a herd of sheep in the dooryard. Each man threw a sheep over his shoulder and hustled back to the truck. They tossed the animals in, closed the high tailgate on them, and then moved on.

"Would you look at those lousy buzzards?" I exclaimed. "They just stole a bunch of sheep from that farmer!"

"That is awful!" Hornsby grumbled, in mock horror. Then we looked at each other and laughed. There had been many a time when we would have done the same thing if we'd thought there was a chance of getting away with it.

Neither of us saw our Albanian come back until he crawled into position beside us. Yes, he had talked to the people the Nazi's stopped. Yes, he had found out what the Jerries wanted to know. They were asking everybody what was the best way to get to Doksat and Kesovrat, the villages we were quartered in, and how far it was and if the road was good. That was all of the report we waited to hear. We sent our messenger packing off to our officers. At any moment we expected to see a German patrol setting out from Argyrokastron and heading our way.

"Hic spate! Hurry up!" I yelled after our departing guide.

Hornsby and I were rather in a cold sweat right then but it gradually wore off as we held our post until three that afternoon with nothing out of the ordinary appearing along the river road out of Argyrokastron. At 3 o'clock a patriot soldier came up with a note from Gary ordering us to report back at once. We needed no urging.

Arriving at the British quarters, we were told that the whole party was moving to a village about two hours away. The nurses and the two American officers had already pulled out and Gary and his sergeants were completing the packing of their equipment. Hornsby and I hustled on to the village where we stayed, carrying orders for our enlisted men's section to get ready for the move and meet the British at the town council house as they came through.

It was nearly dark before they arrived. Gary hired an Albanian kid about 14 years old to serve as guide for us since we were to take a short cut through the hills instead of the regular trail. That was really some rugged going in the dark. We stumbled along, banging into big rocks that rasped skin off our shins and at times stopped us. We fought our way through the thick and briars, with frequent profane shouts of protest as the man in front let a branch snap back to the slash the face of the one who was following. From time to time we crawled on our hands and knees along ledges hardly wide enough for the passage of our bodies, the rough shoulder of the mountain crowding us from one side and a sheer drop of unknown depth on the other. It was a nightmare of effort that seemed never to end and when, suddenly, we found ourselves at our destination, we were amazed to learn that it was still early in the evening.

"Wake me up when the bells ring out and the shooting starts," said Jim Cruise as he flopped down on a stone doorstep and fished his pockets hopefully for an overlooked bit of makings for a cigarette.

"What shooting? What bells?" Paul Allen snapped up the bait quickly.

"It's New Year's Eve, you dope!" Cruise cackled in a good imitation of the old time radio favorite, Ezra P. Waters broadcasting from his station at Rosedale. We tried to get a laugh out of it but were too tired to do much with it.

"So what?" growled Paul. It was just another night in Albania for us. But in the little play of words there flashed across our minds the New Year's Eve at home, the lights, laughter, girls, food, drink, dancing, the funny hats, the paper horns, streamers of bright colored tissue floating over the celebrating crowd, confetti showering everyone as the hour of the New Year struck. But there we were in the night and the cold, tired and hungry. The only lift we got, and after all the one we wanted most right then, was that we seemed to be welcome in the town of Saraginishte. Our hosts acted as though they were really glad to have us with them and broke all records for hospitality.

January 1, 1944, Saturday - Saraginishte

January 1, 1944 found a good many of us attending church services, accompanying the people whom we were staying. We were glad of the opportunity to go, and there was always the prospect of getting a little of the holy bread which was supposed to bring balm to our spirits and was certainly a most welcome change from our almost steady diet of corn. Here, the priest gave us loaves. We were all rich beyond price!

In the evening we were summoned to Thrasher's quarters, where the entire party assembled and exchanged greetings and wishes for the New Year. The wishes all carried the same thought, "I'll be seeing you in the USA!" That was the best wish anyone could make us. At least, when we were ready to depart for our billets, Thrasher told us to be ready to move within twenty four hours. He said that word had been received that the way to the sea was again open and that we might as well forget about the planes. Our way, he said, would take us back through Progonat and Kalonja, through the pass where the Germans had stopped us.

The food in this place was good and seemed to be plentiful. We were like a bunch of starved hogs.

January 2, 1944, Sunday - Saraginishte

On January 2 we had a big day. We were called into British headquarters, given some more new clothes and along with them some dehydrated food. The stuff had been dropped by parachute at Shepr and Major Tillman had sent it over to us. In the afternoon nearly everybody in the party, nurses and men, spent some time taking baths, the first real baths we'd had since we left Sicily.

Most of us had native soap, given us at various places. Hayes and I were quartered in a small room with a tiny fireplace. The Albanian women heated the water for our baths elsewhere in the house and then brought it to our room. We had a good scrub. With our new clothes over our clean bodies and the inner man well satisfied for the first time in weeks, we felt like a million bucks. Late in the day we saw Thrasher start off with Steffa, who was carrying Mohamet's rifle, and our own departure was set for the following morning. Our advance party was to keep ahead of us, making arrangements and paying for the billets and food, thus doing away with the delay of meeting with the head men of each village as we arrived and going through a conference with them.

January 4, 1944, Tuesday – Leaving Saraginishte

If our Albanian hosts were glad to be rid of us, they are surely the best actors in the Balkans. They gathered around us at the assembly point on the village square, shaking our hands, talking to us, some of them even in tears. It was so unusual that we hardly knew what to make of it. If we had saved the town from the devil himself they couldn't have made more over us. But at last Gary was ready and we hit the trail. Looking back from the rising ground at the edge of the village, Paul Allen said, "I want to remember how this place looks." He sighed heavily. "God," he went on, "I'd have to get me a purge of some kind if we'd stayed there a couple more days, all that food!"

"You won't need any pills from now on," somebody reminded him.

"Yeah," mused Paul, dolefully, "cornbread and goat soup."

It was hard to dent our good spirits that morning. The sun was out and the going was good. But in our minds there was the thought of the way ahead. We knew there were two main roads, both under patrol by German troops, forming barriers to our route; we knew there were several mountains to cross. Part of the route we had covered before. We knew it had plenty of bad spots. In some of the villages we were to pass through, the pro-Nazi element might be in control. These were sinister forebodings, but like solders the world around and through all wars, we had come to live mainly in the moment and take our steps one at a time. This morning we were going on, determined to get through, our disappointments pushed into the background.

Hour after hour we marched along; the rest and the food of the past few days reviving our strength and helping us make better time. In a small village, where we had once stopped for dinner, we halted to allow our mules to catch up. While we loafed, Lt. Elna Schwant took a large piece of corn bread from her bosom and declared she was going to divide it with us if someone would loan her a knife. Johnny Wolf obliged and, placing the cornbread on her thigh, Schwant began sawing at it vigorously. Suddenly the knife broke through the crust and went right on down into her leg. Bread and knife slipped to the ground as the nurse stated in surprise at the blood soaking into a dark stain on her slacks. Markie, aided by Sgt. Hayes, was busy in an instant with her first aid kit and they quickly patched up the cut. Johnny retrieved the knife and the bread.

"Sgt. Wolf requests the lieutenant's permission to continue," he said, in his best military manner. Schwant made him a mocking face and then smiled.

"Carry on, sergeant," she said briskly, then added, "I should have remembered that you are butcher-in-chief for Albanian American expeditionary forces."

We ate the cornbread, put Lt. Schwant on a mule over her protests that the wound was nothing, and carried on. At one o'clock we came to the village where C.B. had paid for food and quarters for us, just four hours ahead of schedule. Our plans were therefore changed and we decided to shove on instead of putting up for the night. Gary was of the opinion that we would do well to take the next lap of our route in darkness since it included the crossing of a river and one of the main roads. We had dinner at about three o'clock and at five we were ready for the trail again.

Dusk was falling as we moved out of town, working down the mountain side and into the valley. Two hours later we were along the river, scattered out as usual, the foot troops groping along ahead and behind us, no one knew how far, the mules and a few stragglers. Overhead, heavy cloud banks were drifting and above them there was a bright silver moon. The woods were wet and occasional showers fell in the periods of dense blackness. Gary had warned us against loud talking and had issued orders against smoking or the striking of a light for any purpose.

A barge was to ferry us over the river at the same point where we had previously crossed, but in the dark I don't think anyone recognized the surrounds except possibly Gary and the guides. As the head of the column reached the landing they waited for the balance of the party to arrive and gradually, by groups, we assembled until, counting around we found that only four were to come up with the mules and their Albanian drivers. We sat there in the tiny opening. The moon was clear for the moment and its pale light sifted down through the trees to splatter the soaking ground. Our whispering sounded quite loud in the stillness of the night. Then suddenly we froze to silence.

From behind us, along the trail, there had been the sharp spat of a rifle shot. We held our breath. Another shot stabbed the utter quiet of the night and then, immediately, there came a third. Nobody spoke. Gary's dark form rose quietly form the place where he had been sitting. He stood motionless, listening. Fear took a cold, hard hold on us. What had happened we did not know; but the shots could not be considered a good thing. In every town we had visited there had been the chance that we might be sold out to some Nazi patrol. It was bound to happen. A whisper came from Gary.

"Baggs, not here is he?"

"No sir," someone replied.

"He's got a gun," somebody suggested.

Gary didn't speak for a moment. Then he said,

"They wouldn't give him a chance to use it."

It seemed the only answer. Who'd be shooting back along our trail except Germans? The dark woods around us came alive with

16 – Meeting American Captain Smith

January 4, 1944, Tuesday – On the Trail to Midhar

Off in the darkness of the woods we could hear movements, drawing closer to us. We waited, tense and alert, for a word from Gary. If we scattered quickly there might still be a chance for some of us to escape. We didn't relish the idea of plunging off into the unknown woods with an unknown number of armed Nazis on our trails. But neither did we like the idea of being caught at this stage of the game. Gary darted to the edge of the river, his figure a black silhouette against the dull silver of the water. Then, while he stood there an instant, we heard a voice from down the trail we had come.

"If we had some dogs we'd have a coon hunt if they were any coon around here. Damn good night for it."

The words blew the valve on the tension we had build up and it escaped in a soft, profane murmur of disgust from a number of the boys. It was Jim Baggs. In a very short time he and our other three missing members came walking into our rendezvous.

"What about those shots?" Gary questioned, curtly.

"Oh, that was me," Jim explained, carelessly. "I thought maybe we were getting lost so I fired three rounds for a signal."

I wish I could have seen Gary's face. Guess we all expected him to cut loose with a tirade that would have shriveled Jim in his boots. He stood there for a long moment of silence before turning back to the river. We saw then that the barge that was to ferry us across was close in to the bank.

"Come on," Gary said gruffly, "the quicker we get out of here the better it will be for us."

Pandee, our Albanian guide, turned to Bob Owen.

"Your hat," he said, "it would be so easy to shoot at. It would a bad thing if there was anybody to shoot."

Bob had cut the legs out of his discarded pair of drawers and had made two stocking hats by tying up the ends. One he wore himself and the other he gave to Paul Allen. The two hats did make rather plain marks of their owners in the darkness. Bob and Paul both got the idea and shoved the hats in their pockets.

The barge, managed by two natives, had room for only 16. The first party across were the nurses, Jim Baggs and the British. The enlisted men made the next trip. All went quietly and well, except for some wet feet from water in the bottom of the boat. The Albanians came last towing their mules, from which the packs had been removed for the crossing. We repacked the animals and took off through the woods again. Within a short time we came to a small village, hard hit by invading armies, the tumbled down walls of several homes lying silent and full of jagged shadows cast by the moonlight. It was a place where we had stayed once before. We halted and had a few well guarded cigarettes. Bill Eldridge reminded us that this was where he noticed a number of bee hives and began dreaming up some plans to evacuate a scoup or two of honey. But the few villagers who were out to see us kept too sharp a watch.

"Reminds me of home," Bill declared, with a sigh, "only I wouldn't pick a night like this for it."

Gary told us that one of the patrolled roads was about twenty minutes ahead of us and that from now on it was necessary to stay together so that when we reached the road the crossing could be made quickly. He and Sgt. Blondie were to act as advance guard, moving twenty or thirty yards in front, while Jim Baggs and Jock would cover the rear at about the same distance. In this formation we pulled out of the village and made our way downward into the valley, towards the road. Everything was quiet, save for the faint shuffle of our feet and the soft clop of the mules on the surface of the trail. We spoke little and when we did it was in whispers. Inside I could feel the spring winding up again as we neared the crossing. I was thinking back to that open space we had crossed with Hassan and his guerillas watching from the hills. It seemed so long ago. We'd been lucky then. We'd been so damned lucky all the way. It couldn't hold forever. But I was praying that it would hold tonight.

It did. The road lay dark and deserted under the blanket of heavy cloud that had now blacked out the moon. We scrambled hastily across it, took cover on the other side and pushed along until we reached a small gully, out of sight and earshot of the road. Here we halted to catch our breath, light smokes and talk for the first time that night in normal voices.

At midnight we approached the village that was to be our stopping point. With the hamlet in sight, we halted on a little knoll and Pandee sent a wild Albanian "halloooo!" down to the silent town. Meanwhile, Mohamet and the rest of our natives seated themselves in a group on the ground and began singing their Albanian war chants. It was a scene to remember. The dark knot of figures, swaying as they chanted the strange garble of words that had no meaning to us made us feel that we were witnessing something from the Stone Age. Pandee joined them, between efforts to rouse somebody in the village.

"That's great," Gary commented with deep sarcasm at the end of ten minutes with no apparent results. Pandee paid no heed, eagerly resuming his place among the chanters. By this time rain was imminent and we were ready for assault with intent to do great bodily harm on any and all natives of Albania. But at last two men came out from the village. It was arranged that the nurses, Baggs, and the British would spend the night at this place while Mohamet took the rest of us on to another town about an hour away.

We took the news in glum silence and watched the group move into the village. The long hike had about done us in, and some, who were wearing new shoes, had painful blisters. We took the trail, grousing about our bad luck and grumbling about things in general, as soldiers will, but still making progress. Mohamet dropped behind us, complaining of feeling sick. The rain held off but we were in almost pitch blackness, holding the trail more with our feet than by sight. We got into the village several minutes ahead of our guide and when Mohamet finally came up he threw himself on the ground, groaning. We were in no mood to give him sympathy.

"Get on the beam!" Paul Allen yelled, "We want to take the weight off our dogs and get some sleep!"

"So sick, oh, so sick," moaned Mohamet, lying on his back and flapping one foot up and down. "What to do, what to do," he muttered.

"Holler for the headman!" Paul advised, in a tone that should have tumbled the whole town council from their beds.

But Mohamet only rolled over onto his side and drew his knees up. Meanwhile Eldridge and Ebers had found a large patch of dried weeds, gathered them, and soon had a roaring bonfire going.

"If this doesn't bring them out," one of the boys suggested, "we'll start burning their damn town down."

Within a few minutes some of the villagers appeared, but none of them could speak English and Mohamet, the only one of our party who could talk to or understand them, was still a groaning heap. We finally got the guide to sit up and talk to the town chief. The boys grouped themselves around the fire and a few made attempts to get some songs started; others were giving their opinion of Albania and Albanians without much restraint in either their terms or their voices. While the conference went on, it began to rain. More townspeople came out to join in the parley. We had been in this place before, and had made no great hit, so we didn't expect much in the way of attention. But at last Mohamet completed the arrangements and we began to get moving, in pairs and threes, to our billets. The last ones to leave finished putting out the fire, which had been beaten down to a smudge by the rain.

January 5, 1944, Wednesday – To Golem

Our goal for the following day was Golem. We had been over that trail before and knew it would be tough going. It was still raining when the other section of our party came in and waited for us at the village square. As we left our billets there were occasional flashes of lightning and the rumble of thunder sounded from the mountain over which our trail led. As soon as the nurses and British saw us leaving our billets they moved on, knowing that we would soon catch up with them. And in spite of the weather and a hard day ahead of us, we enlisted men were in a happy mood. The rain increased as we moved up the slope of the mountain and we were soon drenched. Here and there, along the way, we passed the carcass of a mule that had given out and died on the trail. It was another example of the way the little animals were treated by their Albanian masters.

"Work them until they drop, then throw them away," was Cranson's comment.

"They don't throw all of them away," declared MacKinnon, pointing to the mule we were passing. A patch of skin had been laid back on the rump and a square of meat carved out. "I had a piece of that for breakfast."

"Alas poor Yorick," mused Jim Cruise in hollow accents. "Another month of this and you'll leave the mortal remains of James P. Cruise thus upon a lonely mountain trail. Only," he went on, with mock sternness, "I don't want any of you buzzards cutting me up for roasting meat! Leave me to the fowls of the air and the elements so when you come by the place on your fourth trip around Albania with your long white beards flapping in the breeze, there I'll be, just a little heap of white bones. So then you'll stand there, tottering back and forth on your canes and you'll say, 'there's Jim Cruise, the luckiest man ever to set foot in Albania, starved to death thirty years ago.' But don't let me hear you say 'I had a piece of him for breakfast back in '44,' cause if you do I'll rise up and _____."

"Shut up, you GD fool," somebody burst out, "Do you want to hex this whole outfit? We're walking out of this hell hole alive and we're on our way right now!"

Jim laughed until he nearly dropped. We were beginning to think he'd gone off the deep end and we'd have to slap him out of it.

"OK," he said, breathless, "next dead mule we come to I'm going to do the grave digger scene from Hamlet."

"Over my dead body, by God," declared the sergeant who had interrupted Jim's soliloquy. Cruise nodded approval.

"One ass is as good as another," he mocked, "and you'll take a lot less digging."

"Break it up! Break it up!" pleaded Paul Allen earnestly.

Jim obliged by keeping further thoughts to himself and we plodded on, more or less in silence. No more dead mules appeared, and as we climbed higher, the rain turned to sleet, giving us something else to think about. The sleet continued until we reached the village of Golem, about one o'clock in the afternoon.

Nurse Tacina's ankles were badly swollen from the long hike and only her sheer grit and wonderful courage had kept her going. By the time we reached our destination she was hardly able to walk. Lt. Thrasher and Steffa were in Golem and were very much surprised by our arrival since they had not expected us until late in the next day.

The party was divided into three groups, the nurses in one, officers and British in another and the enlisted men in the third.

As we waited, I said, "Well boys there's where we stay."

I pointed to a house well up along the mountain, barely visible in the rain and sleet. Hayes wiped the chill drops from his whickers and he looked up where I was pointing, the sleet striking the point of his cap and bouncing off to pepper his nose.

"Must be," he agreed, "I don't see anything any further away."

Our wisecracking came through with a bang. Within the hour we were on the doorstep of that house, shaking hands with an old man and a middle aged fellow who might have been his son. They owned the place and were our hosts for the night. Once inside, Paul Allen and I, by common impulse, headed for the kitchen, lending somewhat doubtful assistance to the two Albanians in preparation of the evening meal, and keeping watchful, hopeful eyes on the materials that went into it.

The rest of the gang was crowded into a small room where a vigorous fire on the earthen hearth was throwing plenty of smoke along with its heat. While they waited for dinner the boys began stripping off their wet clothes, spreading them out as best they could to dry, and occasionally sending a shout out to us to check on what progress we were making. There wasn't very much civilization left in that room when we brought the chow in. The flicker of firelight revealed naked skin and showed bearded faces topped by tousled, bush heads of hair. We fell on food like savages, every man for himself, and cleaning up the pot and grumbling for more.

January 6, 1944, Thursday – Golem to Kalarat

A wet blanket of snow covered the ground in the morning when we assembled at the square. Nobody was talking much and we moved about restlessly, trying to work some warmth into bodies that were chilled by the raw, damp air. Ahead of us lay some tough going and we all knew it. The trail would take us over the summit of a very high mountain upgrade, with slush under foot. Mules were packed and with the usual amount of shouting, slapping and occasional kicks, got under way with their loads. We took off after the caravan, quickly catching up, and going out in front. Nurse Tacina set out on foot with the rest of us but soon was forced to give up and take to a mule. For two hours we climbed steadily. The snow became drier as the cold increased. It balled on our shoes, making them slip, and clung to our pant legs and melted until we were soaked to the knees.

A drear, sullen wind began to blow; rolling darkness before it that was thick with snow. Minute by minute the smother of flakes grew and the wind rose to a how. The snow began to drift rapidly and at times we were knee deep in the icy fluff, plowing doggedly forward, our heads bent to protect our faces from the blast. Long ago the summit of the mountain, which had seemed close, had been blotted from sight. I followed the gray shapes of the people ahead of me on the trail, once in awhile glancing back to make sure the others were following. I think we all felt the necessity of keeping contact. Then suddenly, close by, as I floundered through a particular deep drift, I heard a voice say,

"Here it is again! This is where I came in from before!"

I knew what he meant a moment later. There was the party, halted in the snow, guides seated in gray knot against the white, mumbling an Albanian war chant, singing it low, almost as if to themselves. We were right back where we had been weeks ago, lost in a blizzard on top of a mountain. The natives didn't seem to be worried much, but they obviously didn't know which way to go. Between the chants, they'd talk among themselves. We hoped that they were trying to argue out the best course to take, but for all we knew they might be discussing this year's crops. The rest of the gang pulled in and joined our circle.

Paul Allen took in the situation as he arrived and voiced a deep disgust that we all shared. There was nothing to talk about. We'd all been through this before. Like being in a fight, having come through once, we had more or less confidence that we could do it again. We swung our arms and stamped around in the snow, waiting the guides out as best we could. After some more chants and additional talk, the Albanians got up and started on through the storm, moving very slowly. We followed, perfectly sure that they had no more idea of where we were going than we did, but knowing for sure that we had to go somewhere.

The next three hours were about as rugged as any we had. Our guides had reason to hold council and go slowly. There were places on the trail where a sudden slip of the foot or an unguarded step might have dropped us into a gray, swirling void of snow. We kept very close contact all the time, moving at snail's pace, safety being our only consideration. Every step took such concentration that we were almost oblivious to the cold and wet. We were probably not making over a mile an hour. But there came at last a time when we could be sure the trail was dipping downward, and knew that we were over the hump. Death was no longer close under foot. We moved with more assurance, realizing that once more, in the pinch, our luck had held.

Well down into the valley we came out of the blizzard and made two stream crossings. At the first one, Gary and Blondie, who had boots, helped the girls across on several large stepping stones for which they had to make extra long steps. Sgt. Bill Eldridge looked things over and then attempted a running jump. It was a mistake. His foot slipped as he took off and Bill hit the stream with a beautiful splash. He crawled out, teeth chattering from his icy bath while we laughed until we staggered.

"G-g-g-o t-t-to h-h-ell!" stuttered Bill, dancing up and down on the bank. Then before we'd caught our breath, Lt. Gertrude Dawson missed the stone she was stepping for. Gary floundered, trying to hold her up as she fell backward. That was his mistake. Dawson squealed and together they sprawled in the creek, Gary on the bottom. The big British Lieutenant scrambled to his feet, waded out, picked up his Tommy gun and then strode off down the trail without a word or backward glance. He was so mad you could almost see his clothes steaming. Dawson had somehow managed to keep from getting soaked from head to foot, but had to finish the crossing by wading. Blondie helped the rest of the girls across. At the second crossing Zieber and Ebers played gallants by wrestling a fair sized log across the steam but their triumph was short lived because we discovered a perfectly good bridge only a few yards down the stream.

At three o'clock we pulled into the village of Kuc again and here, according to information our officers had, we were to meet Capt. Lloyd G. Smith, an American intelligence officer. Smith had been ordered inland from the coast to take command of the party and bring us out as soon as possible. We made inquiry, but no Capt. Smith was in town. So we decided to push on.

Within half an hour, and by another stroke of luck, we met our man on the trail. As he came toward us, with two native guides, we saw the captain's bars on his American flight hat. Smith was a Pennsylvania man, sturdily built, about twenty five years old, with sandy hair and a huge crop of whiskers. His heavy, sheep lined mackinaw hung open showing a gray sweater jacket underneath and he had a .45 automatic in the holster on his hip. British battle dress trousers and British G.I. shoes completed his dress. We learned that he had already been to Kuc and, not finding us there, had back tracked to see if we had somehow got past him. In rapid fire he had the outline of our story and gave us the first direct news we had received from the outside.

From Smith we got an air view of the attempt to pick us up at Argyrokastron. Our "old man," Major McKnight, had sure enough been on one of those C47's. Not only that but he'd had just about a whole PX-full of cigarettes, candy, chewing gum, drinks, food, medicines, and everything else he could think that we might need or want.

"Boy," Jim Cruise marveled, "we were really running for something at that. I don't feel so bad about it now."

The flight returned to base thinking the Germans had us, all but Major McKnight. He didn't give us up. But they saw nothing of us at Argyrokastron. Leaving the town the planes had come upon a German truck convey and the P38's raked it to hell and back with everything they had. The Major's C47 had caught a shower of 30mm slugs that surprised Jerries had sent up in return, but no one was hurt.

"Paid them off for crossing us up anyhow," Bob Owen declared.

Smith told us, "You're grapevine news all over the Mediterranean front. We've all but been at war with British intelligence because all the dope we've had was just what they wanted to tell us. The day you get back the news wires would be plenty hot, only I've a hunch they're going to keep you bottled up for a while."

"I could stand considerable bottling up," Paul Allen mused dreamily, and we all had a laugh.

Smith's original assignment had been to join the patriot forces in Yugoslavia and teach them the use of American weapons, but he had been temporarily side tracked to help us. We hustled along the trail, gradually stringing out as usual, and talking about the meeting with our new leader.

"I'm sure I've seen this guy somewhere before," Adams said, reflectively.

"Well," said Baggs, "that's easy because behind that mess of spinach he's got a face that looks like a man."

"Cigarettes is what I hope he has," announced MacKinnon, with a view to the practical side of things.

"Small potatoes, Mac," I chimed in, "didn't you hear him say he had three to four cars hid out in the brush a little further on?"

"I didn't hear him say anything about cars," someone said quickly.

We hadn't taken a hundred steps when there, in the brush by the side of the road, stood a car, but it had been all but torn to shreds by shell fire and was only a rusty junk heap.

"Sorry," I said, "my mistake."

"Old grapevine Abbott," Owen cracked. "That sure looks like a bad mistake for somebody!"

It was nine o'clock that night when we arrived in the village of Kalarat where our only welcome was the savage barking of a dog. But Capt. Smith got busy at once and soon had us settled for the night.

January 7, 1944, Friday– morning - To Dukat

Our next days' march started with a stream crossing with crew chief Shumway doing the ferrying for those of the nurses who did not elect to jump as the rest of us did. Shumway did the work with no mishap. Gary had recovered his normal good spirits, but was carrying no more women across creeks. Pretty soon we entered a village and Gary bought us some cornbread. Smith, not to be outdone, also made a dicker for some bread. It appeared that we were the first Americans ever seen in this village and while we sat around gumming our double ration of corn, the villagers gathered to see us. At almost nine o'clock we halted at another town to have supper and then push on.

The start was delayed somewhat because Sgts. Allen, Hayes, Cruise and I were very unhappy about the bowl of rotten olives from which they were expected to make their supper. The four of us marched back towards the square to rout out Steffa and, if possible, have our host shot. On the way we met the village president, who cleared the atmosphere by inviting us to make our meal at his house.

The fare was better, but the quantity still left something to be desired. We were used to that, though, and knew that food was short everywhere. At five o'clock we were fed and back at the square, waiting for our officers. When the three Americans and Gary appeared, Capt. Smith got up on a rock and called us together.

"We've got to decide whether we'll put up here tonight and wait over tomorrow, or go on through now," he said. "I know you've been pushing yourselves pretty hard these last few days and I think it depends on how you feel. The going ahead isn't too easy, thought it's no worse than you've been over, and it's not so very far now. But soon after we leave this place we'll be in pro-German territory and it'll be best for us to do our traveling at night. So let's take a vote on whether we go on or whether stay holed up and get some rest."

Delay, even though it meant a chance to rest, didn't tempt us. We didn't like the town and town didn't give a hoot for us. We voted to keep going. Smith jumped down from the rock and preparations for the start were made. Pandee, who had been with us over many a hard mile, was turning back from here. We said goodbye to them and watched them set out over the back trail. Then, just as we were ready to take off, one of our Albanian drivers, who owned several of the mules, decided that his animals were not to go any farther.

Smith and Steffa argued and pleaded, but the fellow only shook his head. It was plain that he thought we were heading into certain trouble and he wanted no part of it. At last, the native simply turned his back on Smith and started to walk away. He had taken only a few steps when the captain snapped out a word in Albanian. The mule driver froze in his tracks, and then turned slowly to face the .45 service automatic held steady as a rock in Smith's right fist. The eyes of the two met for a moment. Then, without a word, the American made a peremptory motion with the gun towards the mules. The driver moved sullenly over to his place in the caravan. Smith, gun still in hand, watched them set off, the loads swaying with the stride of the beasts, and the heads of the men, outlined sharp and black against the twilight sky, bobbing into cadence to their mountain gait. Smith shoved the gun slowly into its holster. He spoke without turning his head to us.

"Let's go now," he said, quietly.

17 – Rescued!

January 7, 1944, Friday - Heading to Dukat

Darkness came swiftly as we picked our way up the mountain trail, keeping closely bunched and, for this reason, going slower than was usual for some of us. The sky overhead was clear and when the moon came up it shed a shadowy, silver cast over everything, glinting here and there on a bit of metal, whitening the wooden saddle stakes on the mules. The smoking ban was on; we were making a conscious effort to move as quietly as possible, and we kept our voices low for the little talking we did. Although nothing definite had been said, it seemed that every one of us realized that our hand was very close to a show down and that the hours directly ahead would bring the decisive turn in our fate.

As we neared the summit of the mountain, one of the mules balked. Paul Allen and Bob Owen, who were near the animal, saw that it was done in and could not carry on with its load. Quietly they took the saddle off the panting beast and tossed some of the less important of the equipment down a steep slope at the side of the trail. The remainder of the load they carried themselves. Then Paul gave the mule a slap and got it started forward again, keeping constantly at its side and urging it on until we reached the top.

Suddenly out of the shadows ahead came a low pitched challenge, spoken in Albanian. We knew then that we had reached the border of patriot territory and that the dark form of the sentry, with whom our officers held a short conference, was the last of the Albanian guerrillas we would see, if all went well with us. He was standing there at the mountain top, in silence, the moon striking a cold gleam along the barrel of the rifle he held at right shoulder, and lighting up part of his rugged, bearded face. We filed by quietly and, almost at once, began our descent into Barley Com Tar territory. We left behind there at the outpost, the last of the men who were fighting and killing our enemies, and were now among those whom the Nazis counted as their friends. There would be under cover patriots, havens here and there along the way, but aside from these, we had to count everyone as hostile, or at last owing us no loyalty or friendship.

January 8, 1944, Saturday Just after midnight

Leaving Dukat

Coming off the mountain at midnight, we were hungry and weary when we entered our first Barley village - Dukat. Steffa had decided to leave us, although up to this point it had seemed to be taken for granted that he was going on through. Now, it appeared, he did not trust Pandee and was afraid that Pandee might claim he had taken this opportunity to desert the patriots. Then, he said, his home might be burned and members of his family shot. C.B. and Baggs didn't argue with him about it. They each gave him their Tommy guns and ammunition and all the money they left. I suppose we have to admit he had earned it and more. But that Steffa! Even now, we all wondered if he wasn't skipping out because he didn't like our chances of getting through on this last lap. He stood there, flourished his big handkerchief, blew his nose carefully, then said,

"You have now not a very long way to go."

Meals were arranged for us, at a price, in several of the homes and we ate under orders to assemble immediately after at the square. When we got back we found an Italian truck waiting and learned that we were to ride instead of traveling by foot. Just how the deal was made or what it was didn't appear. The truck had sideboards up about two feet and then bows for a tarpaulin but there wasn't any tarp. We clambered in over the tailgate, and there wasn't too much room, but we all knew that there was only one truck and only one trip. Capt. Smith stood at the back and spoke to us briefly. He said the road we were taking was held by the Germans and that they often sent patrols over it. If we had to leave the truck, we were to take to the mountain and if we were pursued, were to keep going up and over it. Once on the other side, we could make our way to the sea. Our destination, if all went well, was a farmhouse which could be reached in a comparatively short time.

The vehicle lurched forward and began to roll slowly down the road.

"Well," observed Shumway, in the darkness, "I'm in damn site better shape for jumping that I was the first time I rode in one of these things."

About a mile out of the village the truck halted and in a moment two men stepped out from the shadowy bush along the roadside. They were carrying containers of stolen German gasoline which they emptied into the tank of the truck. Then, without word, and as silent as the shadows, they slipped back into the brush again. Our driver threw the gears in and we jerked forward again.

The old truck growled and wheezed down the road, each turn of its wheels bringing us nearer to that farmhouse Smith had told us about. The road was perfectly straight, fairly smooth, but with dips and hollows that caused our vehicle to sway and lurch, throwing us back and forth as we stood in our crowded positions in the back. After perhaps half an hour, during which most of us were dozing on our feet, word came back that snapped us alert,

"There's a light showing ahead!"

The hoarse whisper ran quickly back through the gang. Those who were in front watched that light down the road, and reported,

"It's getting closer and bigger."

Capt. Smith was down in the cab with the driver. We knew that he too was watching that light, making up his mind what to do about it. There was no doubt in our minds but that it was a German patrol car and that when the distance between it and our truck was swallowed up we'd either be prisoners of war or stumbling over the mountain in the dark with the Nazis on our heels. Still our truck rolled on. Word came back again.

"It's not even a mile away; maybe a lot less."

I think probably all of us had the urge to jump out and take to the bushes, but we'd been through enough scrapes to hold off the impulse towards panic, and stick together. Then, suddenly, the truck stopped. At once we heard Smith's voice at the tailgate.

"Everybody get out! Get into the brush, but fast!"

We needed no urging. We scrambled out of there. I ducked into the bushes on the run and went forty yards up the slope until I brought up a patch of briars where I found MacKinnon. All around we could hear the rustle of other groups and not far away I heard Paul Allen.

"Hey! I dropped my hat back there. Shall I go back and get it?"

"Stay right where you are and keep your blooming mouth shut!" Gary said with a sharp command, followed by a murmur of suppressed laughter.

Down the road now there was no light. This meant that the other vehicle, whatever it was, had its lights out and was now probably creeping towards us in the dark. The minutes ticked by while we crouched in complete silence, straining our ears for the hum of an approaching motor. But no sound came and the road ahead, for the short distance we could see, lay clear and empty. Twenty minutes went by, then, off to my left I could hear Capt. Smith speaking in low tones to the driver and the Albanian's slow replies, in a deeper voice. At the end of another ten minutes Smith ordered us back into the truck.

We piled in again and got under way. We had gone hardly a hundred yards when we stopped again and the report came back that the black bulk of another vehicle could be plainly seen on the road ahead of us. Captain Smith again appeared at the back of the truck.

"If they snap on their lights," he said, "hit the brush."

He went back to confer for a moment with our driver. Then the man started down the road towards the silent black hulk that had halted us. We watched him go, and I don't think there was anybody who would have traded shoes with him right then. The man moved perhaps ten paces out in front of our truck. With the suddenness of a whack of a club, the road leaped into a glare of light.

I can't tell much what happened then. Beside me I remember a whistle of indrawn breath; somebody yelled "Jesus!"; and I know now how the skin along the back of a rabbit must be crawling as he leaps for cover in those few split seconds before the sting of pellets rips into him and he blacks out with the roar of the hunter's gun behind him. None of us expected to reach cover alive, or at least not with a whole skin. By the feel of it, the hair on my head was standing straight up.

But, not a shot was fired. We crouched again in the shadows, panting from our sudden exertions, coupled with ragged nerves. Pretty soon we saw our Albanian driver walking back down the road in the stream of light from the other car. He spoke briefly to Capt. Smith and we heard our leader laugh. Then he yelled to us,

"All aboard! Come on! We're getting out of here!"

We came out of the brush and clambered back to our places once more.

"A German truck," Smith explained, "but two Albanians stole it and are trying to get it back into patriot territory. They thought we were the patrol."

So, we began to roll again. For a minute or two nobody said anything. Then a voice came out of the darkness,

"If we don't have the damndest luck!"

"We have the most blessed luck," a girls' voice corrected gently. "It's simply out of this world, if you know what I mean."

There was no reply to that. We rolled on in silence. Mile after mile went slowly under our wheels and the road ahead remained dark. At last the truck halted again and this time Capt. Smith was cheery as a cricket when he came to the back.

"All off," he chirped, "far as we go!"

Loaded with our belongings, we made our way down a well beaten path to the dooryard of a farmhouse some distance off the road. The truck, meanwhile, had pulled off the road and reached the house about the same time as we arrived. Up on the highway then, a powerful light flashed suddenly around a curve a mile or more away and bored down past the spot we had so recently quitted. We watched those lights while the hum of the swiftly moving car grew in our ears. Nobody had to ask any questions about this car. It fairly yelled Nazi patrol from the moment it came in sight until both the sound and lights had faded into the distance. We let our breaths go in a sigh of relief and got our mouths shut. No remarks on luck were needed. Our two stops on that road had cut things very fine.

It was now two thirty in the morning. We rested a little and then pushed off on foot, leaving our equipment at the farmhouse. We were told that it would catch up with us later. The trail was a steep upgrade and we made slow work of it, resting frequently, but gradually building up the distance behind us. At seven o'clock we were still on the slopes of the mountain.

January 8, 1944, Saturday – 9:00 a.m.

Adriatic Sea In View

Two hours later we at last reached the summit and there, in broad daylight ahead of us, was the sea! Sight of it almost overpowered us for a minute. We simply stood and stared at that patch of open water stretching away to meet in dim distance with the sky on an indistinguishable horizon. Beyond that dim distance laid Italy, beyond Italy there were friends and home. We were seeing at last this goal of days and weeks of striving and danger. Jim Cruise broke our spellbound silence.

"God bless us all this blessed, blessed day," he breathed reverently. But Capt. Smith and Gary left us little time for gawking. It was well someone still had in mind for the work ahead, for we could have stood there for an hour, just looking at the sea and building our rosy dreams.

They started us down the mountain and we soon lost the precious view. The trail led downward on long, easy tangents. There were no villages and we made good time. We were in the highest of spirits in spite of our all night march, laughs came quickly and now and then we started a song. We were going home now, and we knew it. The foot of the mountain was reached at about one o'clock that afternoon and as soon as possible a radio message was beamed on Bari. When the answer came through it told us that a ship would be off shore that night to pick us up.

We moved a short distance back from the shore and away from the trail to a spot hidden from anyone passing that way. Then we settled down to sweat out the hours of waiting. The big question was whether the boat would find us. We worried some about a Jerry patrol stumbling onto our hiding place, but that didn't seem to be in the cards now. We dozed fitfully, starved for sleep, but rousing to check the passing of the interminable hours. The sky was overcast, but it seemed as if the day would never wane. Then, at last, we could tell it was beginning to grow dusk.

Capt. Smith and Gary, who had gone to make arrangements for a boat to take us off to the ship, returned with the assurance that everything was set. Darkness settled gradually over our hiding place, but the arm of the sea in front of us seemed to hold the waning light for a long time. At last our officers were ready to move out onto the beach.

"No lights, no smoking, and keep your talk low," Smith cautioned. We moved out on a shore of gravel where a low ground swell was curling lazily in, and took up our vigil, seated just out of reach of the water, watching the sliding white patterns of foam as the waves ran up the smooth hard sand.

"God, Orville, if that boat doesn't get here," I heard a voice say in the darkness, after a long period of deep silence.

"It'll be here," I said, trying to make it sound a lot more certain than I felt.

"Darker than hell," another voice said presently. "What time is it?"

"Eight thirty two," came the answer, and we sat there, our eyes straining into the murky void in front of us, our ears pricked to pick up any sound. The minutes dragged on. No one spoke again for perhaps half and hour. Then we caught the soft dip of oars and the tiny sounds of a moving boat. A few feet down the beach the black shadow of a small craft slid quietly up on the beach.

"By God I'll row home if I have to," said the voice at my side again. "This is nothing but a damned puddle anyhow!"

"That's right," another agreed, "if I had a board I'd start swimming."

Our boatman had arrived. But that was all. Out beyond was still the impenetrable silence, the age old witchery of an empty sea at night. We waited an hour, then another.

"No soap," a voice sighed, "they aren't coming'."

"The hell they aren't," someone said with a fierce contradiction.

January 9, 1944, Sunday – just after midnight - Rescued

Minute after minute the dark silence mocked us. Not a star showed overhead, not a light anywhere. It was cold and the damp wet smell of the sea was in each breath we drew.

"What time is it now?"

Again the question revealing how tired we had become; not hopeful or dismayed, just tired.

"Pushing midnight and I'm going to throw this watch away!"

I had been dozing; resting my head on my arms crossed on my knees, slipping back and forth between shadow land; but never quite asleep.

"There! Out there! You see that?"

My head flipped up. Out in the murk there was a flicker of light.

"That's it!" The voices were still low, but tense with excitement. "That's her! She's my baby!"

Gary came striding swiftly along the beach, his boots grinding in the sandy gravel.

"All right you chaps," he said, low voiced, "get ready to load. That's our bally boat out there."

We crowded down around the boat where the nurses were already put aboard. It was a collapsible rubber affair and only a few could be carried each trip. When the girls were in Gary stepped into the water.

"A hand here," he said, "Help walk her out."

We fairly carried the little craft off the beach, cold sea water swirling above our knees before we let go and watched it swing slowly to head out into the darkness. Some of the boys claimed they cold see the black bulk of the boat, standing off shore. In about fifteen minutes the boat was back and the loading continued. Finally the last bunch scrambled aboard from the water without even thinking to say goodbye to the land of Albania. Soon we were along side the ship and clawing our way up the rope nets to where the willing hands of the crew hauled us over the rail. Down through a narrow, pitch black passage we groped and then a door opened and we were in a blinding glare of light where there was a commotion of American and British voices. Almost before we could keep our eyes open, we felt the sudden, powerful surge of the engines and knew we were under way.

After that we simply concentrated on taking it easy. We were too worn out to get much of a kick out of the greatest of all miracles, we were really going home! We were out of Albania; free at least from the threat of Jerries; and all we wanted was a hundred years of rest. We went through the night in sort of a stupor. Less than an hour out the boat began to buck and quite a few of us were sick, including me. The British crew tried to tell us something about a night naval skirmish that we ran out of our way on the horizon, but by that time those of us who were poor sailors wouldn't have given a damn if our course had taken us through action between the combined fleets. The nurses were quartered somewhere below. I don't know how they fared, but we who were up on deck put in quite a night.

January 09, 1944, Sunday – 1:30 p.m. Arriving in Bari, Italy

Morning dawned clear and our first glimpse of the Italian coast was somewhere around Brindisi. As we drew in to the coast the sea quieted down a lot and we who had been sick made rapid recovery. Approaching Bari harbor, we went below and picked up our musettes and such other little stuff as we had with us. The nurses, enlisted men, officers, crew, all crowded the decks for the landing which was made about 1:30 p.m., some eleven hours after we left the Albanian shore.

"There's the old man!" went up the cry as we caught sight of Major McKnight on the dock. In the background was a fleet of staff ears. Capt. Simpson, of our outfit was also there, along with quite a flock of intelligence officers. Going ashore we were whisked into the staff cars and away we went for the new hospital, American built and staffed since the December bombing. We were the first patients in the place.

They kept us at the hospital two weeks, not that we needed it, except Jim Cruise. We found out that Jim had been a walking case of pneumonia the last few days and he didn't get there any too soon. They kept us there for quarantine and also to keep us from the news men. Our story, right then, was one of the hottest of the war. An American party, army personnel, of two dozen operating in German held territory for two months and making their way out was something. However, the nurses being with us made it unique among war stories both then and now.

We set, and still hold, the army record for the longest air evacuation flight from Catania to Bari, and I'm sure that it will stand because I can't think of anyone who would want to try to break it.

There's a little more to tell. I was furloughed back to the states, making the trip by air, snatching a seat on troop carrier command ships whenever possible. Bob Owen, Paul Allen, Adams and I started together, coming out by way of Algiers, Oran, Gibraltar, Rabaut, and Casablanca, where we lived several days in a tent while waiting for a place on a trans-ocean plane. In Casablanca one night we struck up an acquaintance with an air force pilot. We sat there, shooting the breeze, telling him we'd just got clear of Albania after being forced down in early November. He said he'd been on a flight that raided a German airfield in Albania about that time.

"Did they smoke one of your ships?" we asked him.

"I'll say," he grinned back. "Mine."

"I'll be damned," I said, and looked at the boys.

We sat a moment in silence. For all of us, there was again the sight of those roaring, speeding planes over our heads on that day so far, far away now. We heard again the crump of their bombs on the Nazi field. We felt the sink of our hearts at the plume of black smoke streaming from one of the ships.

"Guess we prayed you back," Owen mused. The flyer met Bob's eyes soberly.

"We were doing some ourselves," he said, "but thanks for the support."

Late that night in the tent I heard a scuffling over by Allen's bunk. In the light of my flash I saw Paul on his hands and knees in the sand.

"Are you playing mule? I asked, with what I fancied was a fine tone of sarcasm.

"I lost my fifty caliber shell," he answered, "hold your light down here."

I knew what he meant and rolled out to help him. He was looking for the bullet he had picked up from the road out of Berat the day the Nazi fighters strafed us. We pawed the sand for fifteen minutes but failed to turn up the souvenir.

"Now," Paul complained, as he settled himself back on his cot, "I won't have anything to remember Albania by."

I haven't anything either. And with every passing day it all slips more and more into a dimness that is like something dreamed.

(Above) A C-53 Transport Plane similar to what the 807th MAES flew.

(Below) The four-man flight crew of the MAES flight, Lieutenants James Baggs, and Charles Thrasher, and Sergeants Richard Lebo, and Willis Shumway.

(Above) Bordering Yugoslavia and Greece, Albania is just across the Adriatic Sea from Italy. Bari, the planned destination for the flight, is located just above the Italian heel.

(Below left) Clint Abbott and Harold Hayes (fall 2003) look over a map of Albania, discussing the "long winter walk" of the 807th MAES.

(Right) Clint Abbott with Harold and Betty Hayes (fall 2003).

(Above left) Sgt. Lawrence O. Abbott was awarded, (as was all those in the 807th MAES), the U.S. Late Arrival Club Winged Boot. The Late Arrival Club limits its membership to those who have "walked back" after being forced down in enemy territory. (Above right) Sgts. Robert Owen and Lawrence Abbott stationed in Florida following their return to the States.

(Below) The "Late Arrival Club" Winged Boot.

Albanian Villages, Cities, and River Crossings along
Escape Route, 1943-1944. Courtesy Agnes Jensen Mangerich,
Albanian Escape

(Map opposite page) Many of the towns and villages visited were very small, with only a few houses, and they were too numerous to note in this map. They are listed here in order of the party's escape route and lie between the cities and locations marked with asterisks, which do appear on the map. Courtesy Agnes Jensen Mangerich, Albanian Escape.

Editor's Note: Often the nurses and enlisted men were billeted in separate but nearby villages.

Crash site south of Elbasan*

Pashtrani

Berat*

Matishave

Bargulla

Dobrusha

Derzhezha

Leshnija

Mt. Tomorrit* (alt. 8136 ft.)

Terlioria

Lovdar*

Krushove

Gjergievice

Panerit

Osum River*

Gostomicka/Costomicka

 [spelling used interchangeably]

Malinj

Odrican

Permit on the Vjose River*

Mt. Nermerska*(alt. 8186 ft.)

Shepr

Gjirokaster/Argyrokastron*

[used interchangeably]

Mashkulon

Zhulat

Progonat

Golem*

Kalonja

Karla

Doksat

Saraginishte

Drin River*

Midhar

Golem*

Kuc*

Kalarat

Terbaci

Dukat*

Seaview*

Sea Elephant*

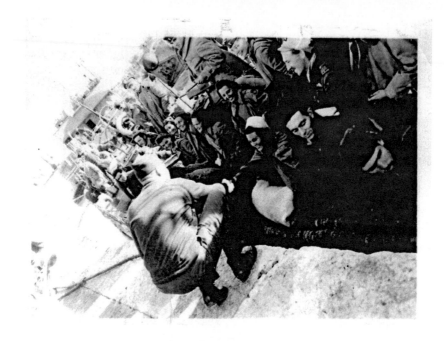

(Above) The 807th MAES arrive in Bari, Italy, greeted by Major William McKnight (kneeling)   (Below) Members of the 807th MAES were welcomed with hot coffee on their return to Bari.

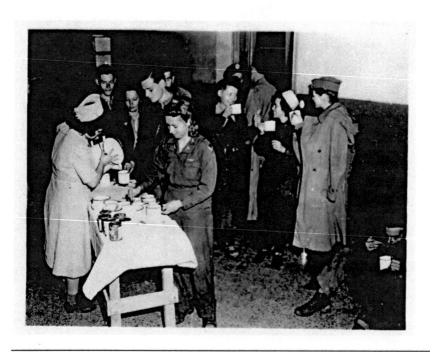

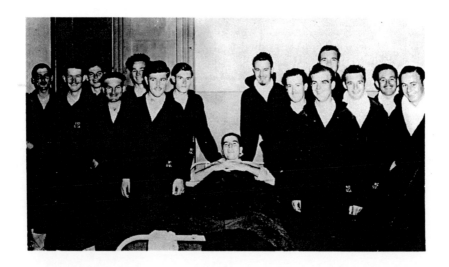

(Above) The enlisted men left to right: Gilbert Hornsby, Dick Lebo, Charles Adams, Bob Cranson, Willis Shumway, Paul Allen, Bill Eldridge, Jim Cruise (in bed), Bob Owen, Harold Hayes, Gordon MacKinnon, Ray Eberg, Larry ("Orville") Abbott, Charles Zeiber and John Wolf.

(Below) The nurses, (Front Row L-R): Gertrude "Tooie" Dawson, Elna Schwant, Lois Watson, Lillian Tacina and Ann Kopsco. (Back Row L-R): Ann Markowitz, Frances Nelson, Agnes "Jens" Jensen, Jean Rutkowski, and Pauleen Kanable.

(Below) The letter that was sent to Larry Abbott in 1945, granting
Larry Abbott approval to publish his manuscript.

284

SEP 24 1945

Power

HEADQUARTERS
591st AAF Base Unit
(1st M-A-T GP)
FERRYING DIVISION, ATC
Stockton Field, California

COM/PRO/GMC/rh

18 September 1945

SUBJECT: Story Clearance

TO   : Review Branch, WDBPR, Pentagon Building, Washington 25, D.C.

    1. Transmitted herewith is a story written by S/Sgt. Lawrence
O. Abbott, 16011035, of this command.

    2. It should be noted that all names of underground (Albanian)
are ficticious.

    3. Sgt. Abbott would like to have this copy reviewed as soon as
possible as he wishes to submit it to several publishers for possible
sale in book form.

GEORGE M. CAHAN
Captain, Air Corps
Public Relations Officer

Incl.-1   1st Ind.   TFP:hs
War Department, Bureau of Public Relations, Washington 25, D.C., 26 September 45.

To: Public Relations Officer, Hqs. 591st AAF Base Unit, Ferrying Division, ATC,
Stockton Field, California. Attn: Capt. George M. Cahan, A.C.

    No objection to publication of the story by S/Sgt. Lawrence C. Abbott,
on grounds of military security or policy.

    For the Chief, Review Branch:

THOMAS F. POWER
Major, Infantry
Review Branch

Incl-story beginning "Benton was down for the
Bari flight and I was posted for Algiers...."

(Above) Clint Abbott meets Agnes Jensen Mangerich at book signing, Riverstop Café, Newaygo, Michigan, summer 2001. Agnes authored the book, "Albanian Escape."

(Below) Clint Abbott and Holly Abbott Bauer pose with Jim and Kay Cruise, Brockton, Massachusetts, June 2003. Jim Cruise was well known in the group for his phrase, "God love ya!" Upon my first phone call to Jim Cruise; Jim said, "Larry Abbott! What a great guy! God love him! If Larry Abbott isn't in heaven then what in the hell chance has guy like me have?"

(Above) Willis Shumay and Clint Abbott meet at the Veterans facility in Phoenix, Arizona, fall of 2000.

(Left) Elna Schwant Krum, Agnes Jensen Mangerich, Clint Abbott and Holly Abbott Bauer, before Agnes' book signing in Newaygo, summer of 2001.

Epilogue

Before I share events that transpired with my Father following his excursion in Albania, I thought that it might be good to share with you, the status of the three nurses, Wilma Lytle, Ann Maness, and Helen Porter.

These three nurses were separated from the rest of the Americans during the German bombing of Berat. While the others fled the city of Berat, Lytle, Maness and Porter followed the advice of their Albanian host and hid in their basement. They continue to live with their Albanian hosts and were assured that they would be rescued.

On January 30, 1944 Major Lloyd G. Smith was given orders to return to Albania and rescue the three nurses. He arrived at the seacoast (called "Seaview") where the others were rescued and then made his way to the village of Dukati. Because of the very active presence of German soldiers in the area, Major Smith and party traveled no further. Messages were sent back and forth to Berat detailing how the nurses would travel. Finally two English speaking Albanian guides assisted the nurse's travel until they reached a house where two British soldiers were waiting.

On March 19, 1944, Major Smith received the message the nurses had arrived. They were pretty good physical shape. They began their final trek home with Major Smith and on March 21, 1944, they too left the coast of Albania by boat, making their way back to Italy.

Sergeant Lawrence O. Abbott, (known to many in the 807th as "Orville", his middle name) after a two week hospitalization in Bari, received a 30 day furlough (as did all the others in the 807th Medical Air Evacuation Squadron).

Sergeant Abbott made his return to the United States by transport plane, landing in Miami, Florida. He proceeded on to Washington D.C., to make a report on his experience and to confirm information already on file with the war department, before arriving in Newaygo, Michigan for his leave.

Shortly after Sergeant Abbott finished his leave, he was assigned with the 805th MAES at Army Air Force Tactical Center (AAFTAC) in Orlando, Florida in the spring of 1944. Another member of the 807th MAES and friend, Sergeant Robert Owen (New York) was also assigned to this duty station.

In Orlando their duties were to fly to ports of embarkation and distribute wounded men to hospitals through this area, and make various emergency flights over the country.

On June 15 of 1944, Sergeants Abbott and Owens were honored with the winged boot, the unique insignia of those who are inducted into the "U.S. Late Arrival Club," a club, formed in North Africa by Army Air Force men for those who "walked back" from a combat flight over enemy territory as the result of enemy action or mishap.

Later in 1944, Sergeant Abbott was transferred to the AAF 501st in Palm Springs, California and subsequently to the 349th at Baer AAFLD, in Indiana (summer 1945).

At Baer, Sergeant Abbott was in charge of a pharmacy in a station hospital, handling prescription fulfillment. He also performed administrative duties in the flight surgeon's office and supply section of the hospital.

While serving at these various duty stations, my father, Sergeant Abbott, began writing his experiences oversees with the 807th. At times, while home on leave, Larry took his hand written manuscript to a local writer, Allen Field Smith. Together they worked on the story and produced a 242 page typed manuscript titled, "Albanian Episode." On September 18, 1945 he submitted a manuscript to the War Department (the Review Branch, WDBPR, Pentagon Building, Washington D.C.).He had contacted a Cpl. Ruth Sprague who served at Moore General Hospital in Swannanoa, North Carolina. She offered insights in how he might construct his writing.

The manuscript submitted used fictitious names for those Albanian Partisans and underground workers who aided them. Just one week later, September 26, 1945, the War Department gave approval for the story to be published. This was intended to be sent to Miss Ann Elmo of the AFC Literary Agency in New York, New York for publication review. What the end result was of this, no one really knows.

The following month, (after serving the United States Army Air Force for 5 years, 1 month and 39 days), my Father received an honorable discharge (October 30, 1945) and rejoined civilian life.

Like so many veterans of World WarII and from a generation that has been recently referred to as the "greatest generation," Larry came back home and joined the efforts of many of that generation in rebuilding America.

While working in the Newaygo, MI area for Mr. Bob Baker as a builder, my Father married my Mother, Verda Crotser on October 13, 1951 and would have three children Holly, Clint (me) and Lori. Shortly after their marriage my Father went to work for General Motors. He worked at the Fisher Body Metal Stamping Plant on 36th Street, in Grand Rapids until he retired in the spring of 1981. During those working years, my Father's devotion to our country was also evidenced in that he took quite an interest in politics, running for State Representative with the Democratic Party in 1960. He did not win, but it's just another aspect of life that showed his love and respect for our country.

As we grew up my Father never spoke of his WWII experiences. What he always told us was, "Don't live in the past." So we never knew much of this at all. We did hear bits and pieces of him crash landing in Albania and walking back, however it was very fragmented and minimal.

As a youngster, I would always go up into the attic and look into his Army Air Force footlocker (which I still have today). Much of his military records were in there, but for a youngster, nothing of "interest" and thereby, we really never knew much of his experiences. My Mother didn't even know he had written an unpublished book until just recently.

One summer night in late August of 1981, I was home from college visiting my parents. My younger sister Lori was there as well. We were sitting in the kitchen, sharing stories, drinking some Cokes, when my Father shared a little more detail of their Albanian experience. He spoke about an Albanian underground group that assisted them. He spoke of the crash and the subsequent help, often times having to sleep in a room with all 30 of the Americans. However, that was about all he shared. One year later, (August 16, 1982) my Father passed away from heart by-pass surgery complications and with him, the details of the story. After he left us, we all went on with our lives.

Fast forward eighteen years to the spring of 2000. While getting the mail at the post office in Newaygo, I bumped into my Uncle George Abbott. He is my Father's last living brother who also served in the Army in WWII. We were talking about how lately people were publishing in local news papers stories like "My Pearl Harbor Days," etc. Uncle George encouraged me to submit an article about my Father's WWII experience in Albania. I said, "Yes, that sounds like a great idea. I'll work on it."

By that September, around Labor Day weekend, I again bumped in to my Uncle George who said to me "how's the project coming?" I started to say "what project?" (I had forgotten about it) but then quickly remembered and said "I'm getting on it this month." Uncle George then said, "You know, he wrote a book about this." I was flabbergasted. "He did? I don't think we have it but I'll look." I then proceeded to do just that.

Living now in the computer age and the age of the internet, I thought I might glean information from a variety of internet sources. Going back to my Father's footlocker, the things in it began to give me better direction of what I might look for.

I found a document from the War Department that had given my Father approval for publishing his story; however no manuscript. I then began to see what I could find about their Albanian experience, if there was any such information.

I opened up a search engine and typed "807th Air Medical Evacuation Unit." I found a note posted on an internet bulletin board that asked the following: "Does anyone have information, have served with, or is surviving personnel of this flight? 'On November 8, 1943, a C-54 ferrying thirteen flight nurses and thirteen medical technicians of the 807th Medial Air Evacuation Transport Squadron from Sicily to Bari on east coast of Italy was forced down...' I am a writer compiling personal accounts of WWII Allied Medical personnel for publication in book form. Pat Sewell, Jonesboro, Georgia."

I read the note with fascination and excitement! I thought, "Wow, this person is writing a book about my Father's experience and needs information." I emailed Pat Sewell and shared my background and interest. She then shared with me that an author by the name of Diane Burke Fessler had written a book entitled, "Voices of American Military Nurses in World WarII." Added to this, I also found out that one of the nurses in my Father's unit had also written a book.

I used an internet search engine and entered "Diane Burke Fessler." In just a few seconds, I was staring at a catalog page from Amazon.com and was looking at the book written by Diane Burke Fessler. Below the description of her book were other book titles that had been purchased by people who bought Fessler's book. One of those listed was a book entitled, "The Albanian Escape," written by Agnes Jensen Mangerich.

I clicked on that book's link and was given a brief picture and detailed information of the book, "The Albanian Escape." The brief summary was fascinating. I said to my wife, "We should buy this book, it has Dad's story in it." I then thought, "Where have I seen the name, 'Agnes Jensen Mangerich?'"

Sorting through old newspaper clippings, I picked up an article from the front page of the Grand Rapids Press, dated Thursday, February 24, 1944. The article, "Missing, Now Safe in State" featured two photographs; one of my Father, Lawrence O. Abbott (from Newaygo), and the other, Agnes Jensen (from Morley)." I thought, "Wow, this is too cool!"

The book review indicated that Mrs. Mangerich was living in LaJolla, CA. I began searching the internet white pages and was able to subsequently locate her number. I did speak with Agnes (who was 85 at that time) and found her memory to be very accurate. We spoke at length. She remembered my Father and provided the names of 8-9 others of the 807th that were still living.

Shortly after that, I met Agnes personally and asked her to sign the copy of her book that I purchased. We had quite a nice visit. Since that time I was able to visit Mr. Harold Hayes in Oregon, Mr. Jim Cruise in Brockton, Massachusetts, Mr. Willis Shumway in Phoenix, Arizona and Mrs. Elna Schwant Krumm living in Hopkins, Michigan.

Each time I visited one of these veterans, I took notes from their recollected stories. I can see how my Father really didn't want to speak too much about the experience. They truly went through some terrifying times.

It was now fall of 2001 and I had not yet located this manuscript or book that my Father had written. Upon a return visit to my Uncle George, I found that my Father had collaborated with a man named Allen Field Smith, a writer for the local newspaper. Mr. Smith had a daughter still living named Marcia. With the help of the Newaygo Alumni Association I located her phone number and address and placed a call to her.

As we spoke, she remembered when she was in high school, coming home and seeing my Father and her Father working on this project together. She also shared that given some time; she might be able to locate that manuscript, thinking it was in some old boxes that had belonged to her Father.

Several months later, Marcia called me and shared how she had located not only the type written work, but also had my Father's hand written manuscript. She wanted me to have these. We made arrangements to get together the next time she would be in Michigan.

On August of 2002, I did meet with Marcia and I received both the type written and hand written manuscripts. This was truly amazing. As I mentioned earlier, until my phone call to Marcia, even my mother had not known of my Father's written work.

Recently, as I was sitting home on Veterans Day (November 11, 2009) I was thinking how many of these WWII veterans are passing on and some with untold stories that should be told. With some encouragement from my friends and family, I pulled out these typed and hand written manuscripts and began entering into the computer for editing and subsequent publication.

I have also used notes from my interviews with some of those veterans who are still living that was in the 807th to assist filling in any holes in the story along with other written works such as Agnes Jensen's book, Colliers Magazine (circa 1944), and newspaper clippings.

Upon editing my Father's work, I used a similar format that Agnes Jensen used in her book and that was supplying a daily date and time stamp upon each new day or location. I think this helps us all have a good feel of where we are in the story.

I want to thank so many that helped put this together. I am thankful for my Father taking the time to write this when it was still fresh in his mind. I am thankful for Mr. Allen Field Smith in helping my Father put the hand written notes into a typed format. I am thankful for the contributions of Agnes Jensen, Willis Shumway, Harold Hayes, Elna Schwant Krumm (who recently has passed away), Dick Lebo and Jim Cruise for their memories of this time in history. I am very thankful for Marcia Smith Klaus (Allen Field Smith's daughter) for sending me the original manuscripts. I am thankful for the help of Mary Jo Hall, a dear friend of our family, who helped review the editing and for supplying recommendations to keep the story flowing smoothly. I am also thankful for the encouragement from my Mother (Verda), my Sisters (Holly and Lori) and my Wife, Michelle. They encouraged me that it was a project well worth doing and helping to bring to completion something my Father started so many years ago.

I am hopeful that this story will help you understand, perhaps, a small piece of the greatest war of the twentieth century and appreciate some of the hardships that others experienced for those of us who live in this great free society called the United States of America.

Glossary

Argyrokastron, is the Greek name for the Albanian named city of Gjirokastër. Agnes Jensen Mangerich uses the Albanian city name of Gijokaster in her book "Albanian Escape" whereas Lawrence Abbott favors the Greek rendition in this book.

Balkans, is a geopolitical and cultural region of southeastern Europe. The region takes its name from the Balkan Mountains which run through the center of Bulgaria and Eastern Serbia. Balkan is a Turkish word that means, "A chain of wooded mountains."

Balli Kombëtar, ("National Front") was an Albanian nationalist and anti-communist organization established in 1942.

Billets, an official order directing that a member of a military force be provided with board and lodging (as in a private home) or quarters assigned by or as if by a billet.

Bivouac (pronounced BIV-oo-ak) traditionally refers to a military encampment made with tents or improvised shelters, usually without shelter or protection from enemy fire or such a site where a camp may be built.

British mission, a designation for any location where one or more British intelligence operatives were "in residence"; the British mission moved from place to place as enemy movements necessitated.

C-53, The Douglas C-47 Skytrain or Dakota is a military transport aircraft that was developed from the Douglas DC-3 airliner. It was used extensively by the Allies during World War II and remained in front line operations through the 1950s with a few remaining in operation to this day

Dysentery (formerly known as flux or the bloody flux) is an inflammatory disorder of the intestine, especially of the colon, that results in severe diarrhea containing mucus and/or blood in the feces.

Gestapo, the official secret state police of Nazi Germany.

GI, General Infantry

HQ, Headquarters

Huns, another term used in WWI and WWII to describe German soldiers. It became less popular in WWII as terms "Jerry" and "Kraut" were more commonly used.

Jerry, Jerry was a nickname given to Germans during the Second World War by soldiers and civilians of the Allied nations, in particular by the British.

MAES, Medical Air Evacuation Squadron

ME 109, The Messerschmitt Bf 109 was a German World WarII fighter aircraft designed by Willy Messerschmitt in the early 1930s.

Mae Wests, Common nickname for the first inflatable life preserver

Musette, a type of small bag

Mauser, a German bolt-action rifle or pistol used in WW2.

Napolean, Albanian currency similar to U.S. Dollar

OCS, Officer Candidate School

Panzer, A German tank. Also used to describe armored military forces, such as a panzer division.

PE-38, The Lockheed P-38 Lightning was a World WarII American fighter aircraft built by Lockheed.

Pill Rollers, Slang also pill pusher (especially in World Wars I and II) the hospital corps, or enlisted men in the Medical Corps

Po, Albanian language which means "yes."

Raki, a non sweet alcoholic beverage served in Turkey and in the Balkans.

Reco, or recognizance is information that is retrieved from an outside source.

SSGT, Staff Sergeant (SSG) is E-6 rank in the U.S. Army, just above Sergeant and below Sergeant First Class, and is a non-commissioned officer.

T-SGT, Technical Sergeant, or Tech Sergeant, is the sixth enlisted rank (E-6) in the U.S. Air Force, just above Staff Sergeant and below Master Sergeant

Tommy-Gun, Thompson submachine gun, invented in 1919 by John T. Thompson and put into use by the military in 1938.

Bibliography

"Balkan Escape." True Comics (Chicago), October 1947 No. 65

"Being 62 Days Late Wins 'Decoration' for Flyers." Yank, The Army Weekly, New York, July 14, 1944, Vol. 3 No. 4

Hayes, Harold (1991). "The Albanian Experience." Unpublished manuscript.

History of Albania. (2010, January 12). In *Wikipedia, The Free Encyclopedia*. Retrieved 00:58, January 14, 2010, from http://en.wikipedia.org/w/index.php?title=History_of_Albania&oldid=337290625

Mangerich, Agnes Jensen Albanian Escape. Kentucky : University Press of Kentucky, 1999.

"'Missing' Now Safe in State." Grand Rapids Press, February 24, 1944.

Porter, Amy. "Balkan Escape." Collier's, 1 April 1944.

Thruelsen, Major Richard and Arnold, Lieutenant Elliott. "Mediterranean Sweep." New York: Duell, Sloan and Pearce, 1944.

LaVergne, TN USA
27 May 2010
184147LV00001B/207/P